Detecting Deception

The Art & Science of Uncovering and Testifying to the Truth

PAUL S. McCORMICK

43-08 162nd Street
Flushing, NY 11358
www.LooseleafLaw.com
800-647-5547

Cover photograph: Inv. Brian Jenkins
Cover concept and design: Bernadette McCormick
Interior photographs: Bernadette McCormick

Detecting deception : the art & science of uncovering and testifying to the truth / Investigator Paul S. McCormick.
          pages cm
     Includes bibliographical references and index.
     ISBN 978-1-60885-069-3
     1. Interviewing in law enforcement. 2. Police questioning. 3. Criminal investigation. 4. Evidence, Criminal. 5. Police witnesses. I. McCormick, Paul S.
     HV8073.3.D48 2014
     363.25'4--dc23
                                                            2013033399

Table of contents

Dedication

To my son, Nathaniel.
I'm watching you grow into an
insightful young man.
You make me very proud.
I will always love you, Big Guy.

Acknowledgments

I have many people to thank.

I would be remiss, if I didn't express my love for my wife, Bernadette, and our son, Nathaniel. You've been very patient and supportive throughout my career. Without question, I love you both. You've put up with my long hours and obsessive qualities. Many times, my job took me away from you (not to mention this book). I'm sorry. You both make me proud. You both make me feel something more than just being a cop.

I owe my parents, Penelope Arms and Donald McCormick, a debt of gratitude. You provided me with the education, opportunities, and emotional support that led to my successful law enforcement career. If I ignored my sister, Abby McKiernan, she'd probably kick my butt; that's written with a smile. I love you all.

To my mother-in-law and father-in-law, Sue and Ed Persina, thank you for welcoming me into your family. I love you both.

I've had the professional and/or personal support of Sheriff Randall Fisher, Capt. Glenn Hanger, Lt. Dennis Back, Lt. A. C. Powers, Assistant Commonwealth Attorney John Reed, Sgt. Aaron Leveck,, Sgt. Darryl Bosserman (retired), Sgt. Bobby Hoy (retired), Capt. Dwight Wood (retired), Paralegal Mary Wood, Julie Hawkins, Assistant Attorney General Phil Figura, Chief Michael Wilhelm, Capt. Becky Meeks, Capt. Thomas Hoover, James Glick (Esquire), Sgt. Brian Jenkins, Kathy Jenkins, Inv. Candace Jones, Dep. Jeremy McManaway, Amy McManaway, Inv. Joey Good, Inv. George Cox, Sgt. Gary Taylor, Officer John Ward, Stephanie Ward, C.I.D. Administrative Support Wendy Thompson, Intelligence Officer Paul Thompson, Jean Sepulveda, A.B.C. Agent James Fetterman, Det. Rob McKiernan, Sgt. Michael Painter, Karen Painter,

Dep. John Larner, Dep. J. W. Wieger, Cpl. Donald Arnold, Sgt. Tony Heflin, Cpl. Derek Almarode, Sgt. Rick Modlin, Sgt. David Lotts, Cpl. Eddie Carter, Dep. Caleb Spence, Dep. Wayne Surface, Det. Scott Thompson, Kimber Thompson, Capt. Kelly Walker, Det. Sue Vance, Cpl. Alyssa Campbell, Det. Ben Lemons, Nenita Fisher-Cromer, John Wells, Courtney Wells, Tara Greene, Melissa Mawyer, Amber Martino, Monique Mims, Pamela Pleasants, Peggy Woods-Kane, Kristen Crummett, Jessica Duff, Megan Marshall, Heather Campbell, Martha Sorenson, Kellie Woods, Grace Werner Ray, Peter Deichmann, Tyler Dodge, James Spurgeon, Bob Tucker, Larry Friedland, Rich Hoopman, Dustin Wright, Audrey Scott, Joan Fink and the many other brothers and sisters and friends of the law enforcement community.

I thank you all

Disclaimer

All the names of the offenders have been changed to avoid any civil issues; most of the cases described are part of the public record. The dates and circumstances are accurate. I've preserved the integrity of the cases described within these pages.

Pieces of a puzzle

Every one of us has a history. Like all people, we're the sum of our experiences. Tomorrow, because of today, we'll either be somewhat the same as or vastly different from what we were yesterday. No one knows what changes that elusive future (that tomorrow) will bring because so much can change in an instant: a death of a loved one, a job loss, or being charged with a crime.

It's the interrogator's responsibility to weave a person's past, present and future together in order to elicit the truth about a specific event, a criminal offense.

Background check

I graduated from Lafayette College in 1987 with a BA in psychology and studio art; my career plan was to go into advertising, to sell people things they didn't know they wanted. That plan failed miserably. From 1991 to 1993, I was employed by the Datahr Rehabilitation Center in Brookfield Connecticut. During that time, I worked in group homes assisting individuals with traumatic brain injury, intellectual disability, schizophrenia, and autism. I eventually gravitated to the more violent (behaviorally challenged) group homes. Those experiences really started my education in the art of speaking with people with active listening, because people in crisis typically respond better to words than to violence.

Active listening is simply the ability to repeat back to a person (who's speaking to you) what he's said, thereby letting him know you've heard him. If you were wrong in what you repeated back, you've at least provided him with the opportunity to correct you. That's active listening: letting the person know (on some level) that you've heard him. We all like to be heard. We're egocentric. If you want someone to like you, you should encourage him to talk about himself. We tend to like people who let us talk about ourselves.

I quickly adapted to different personalities when working outside my previous comfort zones. I was raised in a sheltered, well-to-do environment. It would be accurate to say that I'd been raised in a very privileged environment of country clubs, yacht clubs, and private schools. That previously foreign environment of group homes soon led me into wanting more; I sought greater challenges. Then, from 1993 to 1998, I was employed by the Commonwealth Center for Children and Adolescents, in Staunton, Virginia. During that time, which was arguably one of the most difficult times of my career, I was heavily exposed to suicidal children and children who'd been horribly abused: physically, mentally, and/or sexually.

I was actively engaged. I was genuinely curious. I wanted to learn more; so, I listened. I asked questions. All too often, I became emotionally involved. It wasn't until later (during my law enforcement career) that I became more insulated; I learned to feign emotions instead of actively experiencing them. It is what it is: we all protect ourselves to survive the conditions to which we're exposed. Believe me: I've broken down in front of people I trust. It's rare, but I am human.

In 1998, I worked as a shelter manager at New Directions, Staunton, Virginia, a domestic violence shelter. In 1999, I worked at the Office on Youth, Staunton, Virginia, where I assisted in implementing an intervention program for truant juveniles. Both those experiences further opened my eyes to the world of abuse and violence: Adult victims will minimize the severity of their abuse; abusers will deny their culpability; and repeat juvenile offenders (often the children of repeat, criminal offenders) will blame anyone but themselves for their decisions.

Domestic violence and child abuse/child neglect taught me one of the basic tenets of interpersonal interactions: denial and lies.

We tend to minimize our responsibility for many of our ill-conceived decisions and lie to others about those decisions to minimize the negative responses and/or possible consequences related to those decisions because we want to feel good about ourselves; we *make* our own truth when the *real* truth isn't so pretty. *Truth* can be and often is a subjective term.

When I began my career with the Augusta County Sheriff's Office, Verona, Virginia in August of 2000, I was sworn in as a jail officer by Sheriff Randall Fisher. In 2000, I graduated with honors as the class president from the Central Shenandoah Valley Criminal Justice Jail Academy. I spent a total of 15 months being trained in an overcrowded jail; it had been designed for approximately 90 inmates, and it wasn't uncommon for the correctional officers to be responsible for over 200 and, at times, nearly 300 inmates. That was a brutal education.

There was violence: inmate vs. inmate and inmate vs. jail officer. I'll always remember those smells of feces and urine, testosterone and estrogen. Our balance of control teetered more on communication than physical force. If we had relied solely on force, we (the Deputies) would have certainly lost the ongoing battle.

Sgt. Bobby Hoy had decades of experience in the correctional system, and he taught me the importance of *correctional* balance between verbal and physical control. He was a compassionate man and instilled into me these words of advice: *Don't be ashamed to talk your way out of a fight; but sometimes fighting is the only option, and then you'd better make it a good one.*

I learned; I had to learn; he helped me further understand: There are times (without the overt ability to dominate physically) that the verbal component means nothing. However, ultimately, one's words can exert more authority than the physical force implied behind them, assuming you've earned the physical respect from the inmates. The two did play hand in hand.

Words have more stamina than the body speaking them. In the long run, words have more power.

In 2002, I graduated from the law enforcement academy with honors and spent 3½ years as a patrol officer. Ideally, when fully staffed (which wasn't often), there would be 7 deputies patrolling just under 1,000 square miles with a population of approximately 70,000 citizens. Usually, it was more likely that 5 deputies would be responsible for all the 911 calls. In 2005, I was transferred into the Criminal Investigation Division. For a variety of reasons, I quickly found myself focusing on sex and violent crime, both juvenile and adult. Since then, I've investigated over 400 alleged sex offenses (child on child, adult on child, adult on adult, one variation involving animals, and recently one involving a plant and a child).

I've attended the Reid School of Interview and Interrogation, John C. Bowden's interrogation training, other kinds of training too numerous to mention, and The Virginia School of Polygraph. The polygraph training involved 320 hours of classroom instruction, which covered everything from the history of the polygraph, human physiology, psychology, and the art of interviewing and interrogating. After graduating top of my class in 2007, I spent approximately 6 months interning at the Harrisonburg Police Department in Virginia before taking my license exam administered by the Department of Professional and Occupational Regulations. Capt. Thomas Hoover (Harrisonburg Police Department) was my mentor through the licensing process.

Since 2008, I've been licensed in the State of Virginia as a polygraph examiner, and I'm a current member of the Virginia Polygraph Association. I've conducted over 100 criminal polygraph examinations (for 6 different jurisdictions), ranging from a twenty-year-old cold case murder investigation to child molestation. I'm a child forensic interviewer, trained in cognitive interviewing, a member of our Crisis Negotiation Team, an active member of our multidisciplinary sexual abuse task force, and a Master Instructor for our Blue Ridge Crisis Intervention Team.

I'm proud of my accomplishments, and I know that it was necessary to share them to establish some kind of credibility. However, with all that said, I've had the honor to work with many individuals who have mentored and guided me, and I'll give credit where credit is due throughout the book. I'm not a super cop. When I need help, I seek it out. None of us in law enforcement work in a bubble. For every confession obtained, there were other officers and prosecutors who obtained evidence and information that allowed for a successful prosecution.

I've never interrogated a serial killer, a serial rapist, or a terrorist. Realistically, how many law enforcement officials have had or ever will have that opportunity? For the most part, we're tasked with the responsibility of solving more *mundane* crimes: domestic violence, larceny, malicious wounding, and battery. However, I've obtained truthful confessions from murderers, rapists, child molesters, and other criminals.

I'm not 100 percent; no one is.

In 2011, I was 90 percent in obtaining a confession after a *Deception Indicated* polygraph examination. I've certainly failed to obtain a confession when a confession could have been obtained, and I'll continually lose sleep over those lost confessions. Most of my confessions were **not** obtained after a polygraph examination. I obtained them without it. I've used the polygraph in less than 1 percent of my cases.

I have my skills, but I'm wise enough to watch and learn from others. Just like those suspects I've interrogated: no one is perfect.

Sometimes, I may state something that isn't politically correct; but, in my opinion, political correctness isn't about truth: It's about denial. It's about minimizing. I believe in calling a spade a spade because it is what it is, a spade. I have a passion for eliciting the truth and writing, and I want to share what I know works. It's as simple as that.

Chapter 1
I'm O.K. — you're O.K.

My intentions for this book began as something relatively simple: I wanted to provide the basics for a successful interview/ interrogation. However, during the process of writing it, I realized that I have a very strong opinion: people lie, and we lie every day. I'm not offering that as a bad thing: it's just the truth.

We tell *little white lies* when someone asks us in passing, *How are you doing?* What's the standard response? *I'm fine; I'm O.K.*

When was the last time you responded with, *my life sucks* or *I really need to talk?*

That person asking about your well-being was just following social etiquette; he wasn't expecting anything more from you than that standard response of *I'm fine*; he certainly wasn't expecting to engage you in any type of meaningful dialogue. Furthermore, you understood and politely responded with your understanding of social banter, with that platitude of *I'm O.K.*

We lie to protect the feelings of others. We lie to hide our feelings. We lie to keep ourselves out of trouble. We lie to make ourselves look good. We lie to make others look bad. More often than not, lying is easier than articulating the truth for all the individuals involved in a conversation or social interaction. It's easier to lie to yourself than to accept your shortcomings; most of us think we're smarter and/or better looking than we really may be. We want to hear what makes us feel good; we understand and accept that. So, we lie to ourselves and to others. We allow others to lie to us. A lot of social interaction is riddled with lies.

We lie to children all the time. We tell them: *It's not about winning or losing; it's about how you play the game. There are no winners or losers; everyone is a winner.* What's the truth? Everyone likes to win; no one likes to lose, and there'll always be a winner and a loser when two or more people compete.

Sometimes, we call lies *exaggerations.* An exaggeration is an overstatement, an embellishment of the truth. Once we deviate from the truth, the truth is no longer the truth but (now) an exaggeration, *a little white lie.* For the most part, all lies originate from truth. *Truth* can be built upon lies; statistics are easily manipulated to fit a theory. In today's American society, there's seemingly an excuse for everything and everyone. Those excuses can be considered a form of lying, an attempt at minimizing the ugly truth. The interrogator might as well use that to his advantage.

Questions/Discussion Points

Discuss those "little white lies."
What lies do you tell yourself? To others? Why?

Can a 10-year-old memory truly be an accurate/factual account of events? A 24-hour memory?

Chapter 2
Interviews vs. interrogations

An interview is a fact-finding conversation. You'll want to obtain as much information about an individual and his knowledge of the crime you're investigating as possible. You'll interview victims, witnesses, and suspects; and, all three are more than capable of lying to you.

You'll interview anyone willing to speak with you about the crime you're investigating.

An interview is **non-accusatory** in nature. Even if your *cop senses* are detecting a liar, don't unleash upon the person you're interviewing; he's your friend, at least for the moment. You'll want that person you're interviewing to do most of the talking. Sure, you'll guide; you'll ask follow-up questions; you'll want clarification about statements. Nonetheless, let him talk.

What's our favorite topic to talk about? Me. Me. Me. *I have some interesting stories to tell you about me.* I'll be honest; a lot of this book will be about me. That's just the way it is: we're fans of ourselves. As a species, we're very egocentric. So, try not to interrupt. Make mental notes of his inconsistencies (points you want clarified) but don't interrupt. If the suspect is rambling on about his version of events, he's at least committing to a story. You can always expose any conflicting statements later, after he's fully committed to his alibi.

Talking leads to more talking. As we become comfortable in talking with another person, we unwittingly lower our censors (our barriers) and may inadvertently say something unintended. A receptive audience has a similar affect on the talker as alcohol.

An active listener is exciting to the talker; in response, the talker will talk some more. Upon meeting someone for the first time, if you want him to like you, have that person talk about himself, his favorite topic.

An interrogation is **accusatory** in nature and you (the interrogator) will control the direction of questioning. You'll either challenge or accept the suspect's responses. You'll present evidence. You'll do most of the talking.

There's an art to interrogating people; people manipulate with and are manipulated by body language and with words spoken. People will attempt to hide and/or embellish the truth with the words they speak and/or don't speak.

It's a seductive dance of sorts. Who's going to lead who into what direction, truth or deception?

You can observe this manipulation any night of the week, in your local bar. While talking with a man, a woman may play with her hair. Her actions could be a strong indicator that she's sexually attracted to him. If she adjusts his clothing, his tie for example, that's another strong sexual indicator. She may be doing it subconsciously (because she's genuinely interested in him as a possible mate), or she may be purposefully manipulating that man into buying her a free drink and most likely he will because he'll be responding to her with sexual hopes and desires.

There are ways to persuade someone into accepting your desire for the truth. That persuasion doesn't involve coercion; it's just about subtle physical and verbal cues. On some level, we all have a need to express truth; it's just you're responsibility, as the interrogator, to provide that opportunity to the suspect (the one you believe is lying).

Questions/Discussion Points

How can someone get you to open up and discuss intimate details of your life? You have to be more than just superficially aware of yourself and your "dirty little secrets" if you want someone to open up to you and confess.

Chapter 3
Profiling and donuts are naughty words

We've all formed stereotypes and prejudices; they are the result of our education (schooling, parents, family, and friends) and overall life experience.

A stereotype is the *belief* that someone of a particular appearance or association is capable of certain actions or will behave in a certain way; you see a cop and assume that he's a lazy, bigoted, donut eater.

A prejudice is a *feeling* that someone of a particular appearance or association is capable of certain actions or will behave in a certain way; you **fear** that a cop will beat the living snot out of you because that's what cops do.

We all react to people based on those stereotypes and prejudices. It used to be called profiling. Profiling became a naughty word. I've heard profiling referred to as *behavioral analysis* in an attempt to make *profiling* a politically correct concept. Regardless, we all profile. When you walk into a room of strangers, you make certain assumptions based on their appearance and actions because of your life experience and education. Sometimes, you're wrong. But, if you don't profile, you're ignoring your gut, your primitive brain.

> *You're lying to yourself, if you deny that you profile.*

Frankly, there's absolutely nothing wrong with a law enforcement official (any person) having personal stereotypes and prejudices because all people have them (cops are human); it's the inability or unwillingness to learn from new experiences and education and change accordingly that can be a problem; it's **discrimination** that can be a problem.

To discriminate against someone is to **act** upon your stereotypes and prejudices without provocation, without that person overtly expressing and/or displaying a behavior that could potentially endanger you or others. Obviously, if someone looks and acts like a gang member, you should approach him differently than you would a senior citizen lost in the park.

Actions are the criminal problem in society, not feelings and beliefs. An Officer or Deputy's actions and/or statements are what may result in a confession being eliminated from evidence, not stereotypes and prejudices.

If you want to successfully interrogate someone, you must acknowledge your stereotypes and prejudices prior to speaking with him. Rest assured, they may be valid beliefs, but you'll have to temper them. You'll have to be neutral and nonjudgmental.

It's all about best practices.

No one is perfect, including you. That badge doesn't make you flawless. That's a big mistake a lot of law enforcement officers make when they are interrogating someone: They think they are better than him. I've been guilty of it.

I'm proud of all my brothers and sisters, the good ones. Most are. We all know some who could be better. There are some who should not wear a badge. That's the truth. There are good employees and bad employees in any profession.

That suspect has opinions about you, rooted in his life experience, as much as you do about him. Is it possible that he's had a negative experience with a law enforcement official? Absolutely.

If you discriminate, he'll discriminate. You'll get nowhere in an interrogation. He's a thug; you're a bigoted, donut-eating cop.

If you think all law enforcement are without flaw, if you think **all** criminals are without some redeeming qualities, then stop reading this book.

With that said, I do like strawberry-filled donuts.

Questions/Discussion Points

Discuss your stereotypes and/or prejudices.

What positive qualities can a pedophile have? A white supremacist or a Black Panther? Like it or not, someone in their life will tell you about how wonderful they are/were.

Chapter 4
You ain't all that and a bag of chips...

In any given situation, leave ego aside. If it appears that the suspect is responding to a so-called rookie, you should allow him to take the lead in the interrogation. The vast majority of a successful interrogation is the result of having established a rapport with the suspect. It's easy to forget that you're a flawed human, especially when wearing a badge of authority. If nothing else, we have flawed family members who, despite whatever transgressions, we love because they are family.

I'll always remember my first interrogation. In 2004, I was that rookie. A fellow Deputy, now Cpl. Eddie Carter, and I interrogated a man, Donald Dunivan, who was suspected of maliciously wounding a man (with a knife) during a party.

It had been one of my first man hunts, a man with a weapon on the run in the community, somewhere in a subdivision, around midnight. It was exciting. Then, there we were, Deputy Carter and I, in the Sheriff's Office with the suspect.

I'd retrieved a camcorder from the dashboard of my car. In 2004 it was before the Augusta County Deputies all had digital recorders and, the Sheriff's Office had an interrogation room with audio/visual recording capabilities accessible to everyone. To activate the camcorder in my car during a pursuit, I needed to lean forward and hit the record button; at that time, nothing was automatic in its response. Now, by activating your lights, the recording automatically begins.

Times have changed. These days, even if you're not recording, it seems like everyone has a cell phone capable of recording. And, rest assured, if people with cell phones can record you in action, they will. They would prefer to catch you violating someone's civil rights.

Regardless, Deputy Carter and I had all the probable cause needed to obtain a warrant for malicious wounding: the victim had identified the suspect; a teenage girl (who'd been the focal point of the conflict) had identified him; people at the party had identified him. The suspect didn't know what we knew because we hadn't told him. He was just willing to talk; he'd made that perfectly clear when I was transporting him to the Sheriff's Office. What's to follow wasn't a result of amazing police work; it was purely curiosity and empathy.

Deputy Carter bought him a soda before we sat down. We weren't accusatory. We'd been establishing a rapport, even if we didn't know that by establishing rapport (being respectful) we were increasing our odds of a confession. We weren't judgmental. We just wanted to know why he did what he did. Certainly, my background in psychology was overflowing with questions: What drove a man to *stab* another man?

He'd been Mirandized.

I told Dunivan that I knew he'd cut the victim; there was a reason he was here *now*; there was a reason he was in custody, and I wanted to know *why* he did what he did. I wanted him to help me understand what had happened, his side of the story. I asked him: *How did it make you feel when you stabbed him, the victim* (an acquaintance)? His answer was: *It made me feel good at the time; I was angry. It wasn't right what he* (the man he stabbed) *was doing in my house, at my party.*

The victim, a 19-year-old male, had been making sexual advances on a teenage girl who was 13 years old. The victim continued his advances despite Dunivan verbally intervening. Things escalated into a stabbing. Drugs and alcohol were certainly factors in the night's events. The victim wasn't without some culpability.

Deputy Carter and I allowed Dunivan to speak without being judged. Ultimately, he demonstrated remorse by expressing it in the form of a confession. A statement of remorse (an apology) is a confession: *I'm sorry for my* actions. It's a simple idea but an important one: a confession can be as simple as asking for an apology. We all make mistakes, don't we?

His mistake resulted in a 10-year prison sentence.

Unfortunately, the victim received nothing more than his stitches. As inappropriate as his behavior was toward that girl, it wasn't criminal.

A lot of parents can empathize with Dunivan and his criminal actions.

I certainly can.

Questions/Discussion Points

Discuss a situation that could cause you to commit a crime.
Would you steal food if you were hungry?
What if your child was starving?
Could you understand how you might commit an act of violence against someone who raped someone you loved?

Chapter 5
If you didn't do something, how's it possible that you were seen doing it?

In 2009, I had a case involving a grandfather, Barry Johnson, who was accused by his 7-year-old granddaughter of molestation. These incidents of molestation occurred while he sat in front of the computer, in his family common room. She described images of naked adults on the computer monitor while Johnson digitally penetrated her.

I interrogated him, but he never confessed to molesting her, of putting his fingers in her vagina.

But, he was willing to talk—so, I let him talk. Then, in court (during a jury trial almost a year later), there was a pivotal moment. The assistant commonwealth's attorney, John Reed, asked Johnson if he'd ever masturbated in front of the computer. He replied that he **never** had.

I was called as a rebuttal witness; I never expected to testify because Barry Johnson had never confessed. However, I'd been sequestered just in case he testified and made any statements that I could refute. Now, I was on the witness stand and Reed asked me if I had the opportunity to speak with the defendant; I stated that I had. Reed asked if the defendant had made any statements about masturbating in front of the computer. I responded that he'd admitted to masturbating in front of the computer, and all hell broke loose.

The defense attorney hollered about rules of best evidence, and there was some debate. The jury was asked to leave the courtroom.

15

I knew what portion of the interrogation the defense attorney was referring to; the issue was about to become a matter of semantics, language. I cued the DVD to one particular time frame that coincided with the defense attorney's time frame; we both had it written down: 72 minutes.

During a segment of my interrogation, I'd asked the defendant, Johnson, if he'd **ever** masturbated in front of the computer; he stated that he had **never** masturbated in front of it. I asked a couple more unrelated questions. Then I followed up with:

"Is it possible that your granddaughter could have walked in on you masturbating in front of the computer?"

He stated that it was *possible*. He clearly stated that it was possible that his granddaughter could have walked in on him masturbating in front of the computer.

There was only one conclusion I could come to (that anyone could have reasonably come to): he had indeed masturbated in front of the computer. His granddaughter could not have possibly walked in on him masturbating in front of the computer, if he had not indeed been masturbating in front of it.

It was a matter of semantics, and the judge permitted that portion of my interrogation to be heard by the jury. It would be the jury's decision. In my professional opinion, when I answered that question *(Did he admit to masturbating in front of the computer?)*, I was 100 percent honest.

My reputation was on the line. Quite frankly, there had been an error in my interrogation: not noting what he'd said until I reviewed it days later. Had I picked up on his statement when he said it, maybe the courtroom drama could have been avoided.

Maybe that 7-year-old girl wouldn't have had to testify in front of 12 jurors in circuit court. The jury agreed with my interpretation of his statement. His credibility was destroyed, and he was convicted. He received 10 years in prison.

My lesson learned: pay attention to the words, every word. I was so focused on getting the bigger confession—fingers in the vagina—that I missed the more subtle details. At least, I'd kept him talking. At least, I'd recorded and reviewed his interrogation.

Questions/Discussion Points

Discuss the "It's possible" statement.
Is it that much different than someone saying, "Maybe"?
Could something have *possibly* happened or *maybe* have happened if it/that physical act never occurred?

Chapter 6
The voices around me: record the chaos of whispers

Record everything. I have a digital recorder on my belt, and I record **all** my interviews and interrogations. In Virginia, I don't have to announce that I'm recording. Virginia law states that as long as one person, actively involved in the conversation (that's me), knows that it's being recorded, the recording is legal. That's Virginia. Your state may be different. Know your laws.

Even if your state requires you to announce that you're recording, don't make a big deal of it. Approach it as: *Hey, I'm an absentminded fool. I don't want to get the facts wrong in my report. You can understand that, can't you? I want to make sure I get it all right. You won't mind then, if I record us, will you?*

Most likely, he'll agree to the recording. Who doesn't want to be heard in their own words as opposed to the words, in some report, of some cop? After he agrees to it, and you shut up about it, after you discrete the recorder away, he'll forget about it. Quite frankly, I doubt you'd have to show the recorder. If your state requires that you announce it, then, announce it. You don't necessarily have to do a show and tell.

Oh, by the way, here's the recorder. This is what it looks like. Now, I'm pressing the record button.

Digital recorders are small. They are easily forgotten.

Badges are small, too. After you announce your legal authority, you should minimize your legal authority; you should never fully deny who you were before that badge, before you *knew* better. We were all teenagers, once. I remember being a teenager, but I've minimized many of my transgressions as have my parents because of time and disregard, time and perspective. Now, we can joke about some things that were fairly serious at the time, but, regardless, my transgressions occurred; they caused a lot of emotional upheaval. During my teenage years, I was a pain in the ass. My parents may have easily referred to me as something a lot worse than *a pain in the ass*. More likely I was someone needing a pickax and a shovel.

The suspect is no different; he has a past; he has emotional connections to people. It's up to the interrogator to spin his past into the best possible light, whatever *it* may be. Somewhere out there, there are people who know the suspect and that suspect wants them to *see* him better than the law wants to *represent* him. Those people may be his children, his mother and/or father, a coworker, or a clergy member; they may be the murder victim's family.

That *someone* is a person who (statistically) the suspect knew prior to the violent crime, before making that *someone* his victim.

Questions/Discussion Points

This won't be easy and may cause a heated debate.

Discuss how a rapist can be presented in the best possible light. Was the victim was being overly seductive?

I'm not excusing rape, but did the victim's actions/decisions increase her odds of being raped?

Chapter 7
How you ask a question can affect how a person will answer that question

Most cases don't wind up in court for months, sometimes more than a year after the arrest. Don't give the defense attorney any wiggle room. The defense will argue every aspect of your report, as he should. That's his job: to keep you, us, honest. *Can you be sure? Are you sure? How can you be sure?* He'll ask a litany of questions to introduce doubt into the judge or jury. Let the audio tell the story. Shut the defense down.

Miranda is often attacked by the defense. My interpretation of the Supreme Court decision regarding Miranda, which is founded in conventional wisdom, is that Miranda applies when you have someone in custody, **and** you are questioning that person (*Miranda v. Arizona*, 384 U.S. 436 *1966*). You don't have to read Miranda, if you **do not** question the person who's in your custody. If you're recording **and not** questioning the person, any statements he makes are admissible in court as *spontaneous utterances*.

If you're transporting a person who's been arrested and has **not** been Mirandized, **don't** ask any questions. Quite frankly, I wouldn't ask that person if he likes punk music. *Mum's the word*. If that person makes a spontaneous utterance, it's admissible in court. But, you shouldn't ask any questions (inquisitive in nature and/or related to any criminal activity or anything closely related), because those questions can become a slippery slope for the prosecuting attorney (in trial) if you've asked them. The defense attorney could successfully argue that you were baiting his client into answering questions that led to his client's confession. Avoid those complications.

When Miranda applies (and I'll leave that to your department policy), it's effective to say, prior to reading Miranda: *There are so many things I want to share with you; I really want to hear your side of things; however, before we can do that, I must read you Miranda. So, bear with me,* and then read Miranda.

That **we** in *before we can do that* is important. That simple little pronoun, **we,** implies that you are working together with him; it breaks down that *me **against** you* dynamic. It becomes less about you against him; it's more about us, you and me. You're establishing that rapport. Furthermore, you've baited him with that, *There are so many things I want to share with you.* He wants to know what you know. To find out what you know, he'll likely waive Miranda.

Curiosity is a hard temptation to resist.

Simple little pronouns, like *we,* can make all the difference in what information you obtain from someone. If it's *you against him,* the battle will be fierce; he'll likely tell you where you can shove it. If it's you working together with him, a confession will more likely be obtained.

Questions/Discussion Points

How do you feel when someone judges you? Angry? Defensive?

How do you feel when you're judging someone? Superior? Just a little bit better than him?

Chapter 8
It's all about timing

Custody is considered from the perspective of the individual being questioned. It's not your perspective. Often, during my non-custodial interrogations, I like to slip in, "You're free to tell me to leave whenever you want; or, you're welcome to leave, but I'd like to continue talking with you because I'm starting to understand."

Timing is the key. When the suspect is talking about non-threatening/**irrelevant stuff**, just throw in something that clearly indicates he can tell you to leave, or he can leave. I slip it in about every 30 minutes. It's low key. Quite frankly, it becomes a personal challenge for me: How many times can I offer the *out* without the person taking it, while still getting a confession? It's a game between me, the suspect, and the soon-to-be-known defense attorney. If he's talking about **relevant issues**, I don't mention his options.

In a multi-jurisdictional case, Detective Ben Lemons (Waynesboro Police Department) and I, within approximately 90 minutes, reminded the suspect 7 times that he was free to leave but that we certainly appreciated him talking with us. Nine months later, the suspect's defense attorney, based on his client's information, approached us and stated that his client didn't feel free to leave our noncustodial interrogation. The attorney was going to attempt to have our recorded confession suppressed. Once he listened to it, he dropped his motion to suppress.

If you don't have a rapport, the person you're interviewing will happily take you up on that *out*. For example: If you are in the process of telling the suspect what an *asshole* he is, the odds are he'll take the first *out* you provide him, if not before. Establishing a rapport is not a weakness, it's a strength.

Law enforcement has its weapons, guns and tasers; we have our authority and the ability to assert ourselves and deprive someone of their freedom. More often than not though, by playing *nice* (and by *nice*, I mean not *getting into his face*), you can get what you want (that confession) and the guilty go to jail.

It makes a defense attorney's job a lot more difficult when you've been respectful to his client and have clearly indicated to his client that he was free to leave or more than welcome to have you leave. I'll say it now, and I'll say it later: your interrogation **will** be played for a judge or jury. If you're yelling and screaming, if you're aggressive and hostile in your tone, you may turn the judge or jury against you. Even if you weren't violating the suspect's civil rights, your tone and volume of voice can still work against you. Don't give anyone the ability to entertain the idea that you threatened and/or intimidated your suspect.

Questions/Discussion Points

How do our moods affect others on a daily basis? How do their moods affect you?

Discuss how your tone of voice and your physical demeanor can adversely affect a judge or jury.

Chapter 9
Hunters turn hunted

We may be evolutionarily advanced; however, we still survive (or, at least, we should) by using a reptilian portion of our brain, the primitive brain, the *medulla oblongata*. That portion of our brain is located in the brain stem. It's old, primal, and predictable:

Can I kill it? Can it kill me? Can I eat it? Can it eat me? Can I have sex with it?

It's a lot more complicated than how I'm about to further describe it (because the amygdala, the thalamus, and the cerebral cortex function in conjunction with the medulla oblongata in what is referred to as the limbic system), but for my purposes (interviews and interrogations) the medulla oblongata controls our autonomic nervous system, wherein lies the sympathetic and parasympathetic systems. It controls our involuntary functions such as breathing, heart rate, and blood pressure. We don't have to think about our breathing, our hearts beating, or our eyes dilating; it all just happens, automatically.

> ### Fight, flight, or freeze.

As you get more comfortable with observing a person and his body, practice observing his carotid artery; it's in the neck, right side. If you hit a sensitive area while questioning him, you'll see an increase in blood movement and volume. You can observe that same reaction in the radial artery, which is located in the forearm, the wrist area.

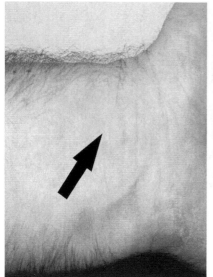

Radial Artery (left wrist)   Carotid Artery

I'll admit that's a little advanced; but the difference between a new interrogator and a seasoned one is not necessarily their knowledge but their ability to use as much of that knowledge as possible when actively engaging someone in an interrogation.

The suspect is in the interrogation room (the woods) and confronted by me (a big bear). Instinctually, he'll do one of three things: he'll prepare to fight the bear; he'll run like hell; or he'll freeze (like that deer in the headlights of an oncoming car), because he's trying to disappear, make himself small/invisible—*Maybe, if I just stay still, it'll all go away.* The sympathetic portion of the medulla oblongata (the autonomic system) prepares him for those three possible responses by increasing his heart rate; increasing his blood volume which is why you may see the arteries when before you didn't; increasing his intake of oxygen because more oxygenated blood flows to his skeletal frame and his muscles; and dilating his pupils to take in more light and information. Blood flow decreases to his stomach because digesting food isn't important if he's confronted by a bear. Once again it's far more complicated, but that information gives you the basics.

When the threat is over, when that bear is gone, the parasympathetic portion of the medulla oblongata kicks in. The suspect's heart rate decreases, and he can start digesting food again. We'd all stroke out if we lived in a heightened state of fear all the time.

> ### *Rapport is absolutely important in obtaining information or a confession*

Confessions tend to secure a conviction. There's nothing better than the suspect stating what he did and why, explaining his motive. That motive can make that difference between a premeditated murder and a murder of passion. And by *stating*, I mean a recorded statement of the suspect giving details of his crime (his thought process) and his emotions at the time of the crime. Premeditation can be formed in a matter of seconds.

You may despise what that person has done, but it's not up to you to condemn him. It's not even up to the judge to condemn the suspect. It's the letter of the law and the sentencing guidelines that *legally* condemn the suspect.

Don't rush things. The innocent will usually tell you when they are done talking with you, after they realize you haven't bought what they are selling, the truth. They'll tend to be rather forceful about their innocence and demand a lawyer and rather quickly.

The guilty are more likely to stay with you during accusatory questioning. They want to believe that you believe what they are selling (their lies), before they leave. They want to believe that you believe them because their successful deception (their free-dom) depends on it.

They are trying to avoid jail; they are trying to reduce their physical and psychological stress. Their denials tend to be weak, lacking conviction.

Questions/Discussion Points

Discuss fear: that roller coaster ride, those near accidents, that feeling of dread when you're called upon in class to answer a question for which you don't have an answer.

Chapter 10
Who knew who and how?

It sounds obvious but, before conducting an interrogation, you should have conducted a *thorough investigation*. Before you accuse someone of a crime, *even if you know he did it*, you should know the details of that crime, know something about the suspect's background, his criminal history, his family, and know something about the victim (his victimology).

Did the offender know the victim? If they knew each other, what was the nature of their relationship? In the vast majority of violent crimes (rape, assault and battery, aggravated battery, murder), the victim knows the offender. So, why did the offender offend against the victim? If the offender didn't know the victim, why did he select the victim? What's the victim's lifestyle, his habits?

It's all about motive. Every last one of us has a motive for everything we do and say. We may not always be conscious of a particular motive, but it exists. Just like we don't have to consciously think of breathing or making our heart beat, we do what we do when interacting with others on some level of instinct. We know how to fake smiles because we understand social and work etiquette. If we tell our boss to screw off, he may fire us. So, we censor our words because we're motivated to keep our job. We want people to like us. When interacting with others we do what we do to minimize negative responses while, ideally, increasing positive responses. We like to be liked.

We're creatures of habit. We do the things we do because we believe that whatever it is that we're *doing* works. It's not that it necessarily works; it's that we believe it works. The suspect has done whatever he has done because he was motivated (at that time) to do what he did because of the circumstances, like it or not.

Therefore, before meeting with the suspect, you want to know the details of the crime and have more than a passing insight into what kind of person he is: Do his friends and acquaintances describe him as a nice guy or as a mean guy? Is he extroverted or is he introverted?

> *An extrovert is more action oriented than emotionally oriented; the introvert is more emotionally oriented than action oriented. You don't want to necessarily discuss emotions with an extrovert.*

Little things like that will give you an insight into how to approach the suspect.

It doesn't matter if you and everyone else in your department find the crime reprehensible (such as child rape) because the offender has his own *valid* reason for what he did, *his motive*. If you take that away from him (his valid motive), he won't talk with you; he won't confess. He'll tell you *to kiss off.*

> *You're simply tasked with obtaining the facts of the case, not to judge.*

Questions/Discussion Points

Discuss motive: theft, rape, murder.
Successfully argue your reasons for those types of crime.

Chapter 11
Reality is nothing more than the personal perception of the physical realm within which you interact.

Abraham Maslow (a psychologist) and Sigmund Freud (a neurologist credited with creating psychoanalysis) presented two theories about the human psyche.

Maslow postulated the idea of the *Hierarchy of Need*. I've simplified his idea because it's the basic concept of *need* that applies to the interrogation: the 1st level of need is food, water, and safety (drugs can easily be considered a need; fulfilling an addiction is a powerful need); the 2nd need is esteem and the desire for friendship, family, and intimacy (how others perceive us; peer pressure has resulted in many people doing things that they might not have otherwise done); and the 3rd level is self-actualization/self-esteem (how we perceive ourselves through a culmination of life experience).

Maslow argued that if the 1st need is not met, an individual will not successfully develop esteem (the 2nd level) because his focus remains on the basics of survival. Think about children from abusive homes: in school, they tend to be more reclusive; they are reluctant to interact with their peers because they have a *secret*. If they can't foster friendship, it's unlikely that they'll acquire self-esteem. One won't evolve into that self-esteem stage, if the esteem level hasn't been fully developed.

Need is simply about psychological and emotional development; one step leads to another.

Maslow's hierarchy of need (in my opinion) is strongly correlated to Freud's theory of id, ego, and super-ego.

The id is primal: I want what I want when I want it. The id doesn't consider the consequence of action. Think about a two-year-old child in the throws of a tantrum. All parents have been in that situation when their child wants what he wants and their child just breaks down. Those memorable moments typically happen in a large store with many judgmental people looking on.

The ego has more constraint; it understands the concept of right and wrong; it understands consequences: if I do this, this may result, for instance, jail. The ego knows that certain acts are considered criminal and have consequences. A child may take that chocolate chip cookie despite being told not to. He's apprehensive (that autonomic nervous system is kicking in) but does it anyway because he wants it (id); he makes the decision to take it despite the risk of being caught. At that time (the wanting of the cookie), his id overpowers his ego.

The super ego is about morals and ethics. The super ego is more highly developed. A person won't steal because he understands that stealing is fundamentally wrong; he has a *conscience* (my interpretation); he intrinsically understands guilt and shame. His intrinsic understanding of *guilt and shame* motivates him away from committing a criminal act. His understanding of guilt is pre-existing; he understands consequences and how his behavior can affect others before acting upon his behavior, how his behavior will affect him. That's different than a person who feels guilt after being caught; his *guilt* is rooted in *feeling guilty* because he was caught and is (himself) going to experience negative consequences (ego; *I've been busted*).

I postulate that self-actualization/self-esteem is similar to the super-ego; esteem to the ego; and Maslow's 1st level (of food, water, and safety) to Freud's id.

Within all those theories lies a person's motivation. It's seemingly convoluted. But, it's there; it's simply there. A suspect did what he did because it was the thing to do at the time. You, as the interrogator, must embrace that; you must accept that. You must weave yourself through those psychological theories (accept them as stages of development, as relatively primitive but driving forces in our behavior) and connect with the suspect.

You shouldn't judge—you're no better than the suspect—if you want a confession.

Questions/Discussion Points

What are your flaws?
What are your weaknesses?
What are your temptations?

Chapter 12
If you come across as perfect, without flaw, the suspect will not trust you.

Our suspect: Where did his motivation for the crime originate? Did he steal food to feed his family? Did he steal money to support his drug habit? One motive is certainly more worthy of compassion, the theft for food; however, it's not for you to judge if you want a confession.

Need is need.

Regardless of the motive (regardless of the nature of the crime) you must establish that rapport. There are two reasons: to detect deception you must have established a baseline for the suspect's behavior and his manner of speech; and, to obtain information, the suspect must like you. By *like*, I mean he must believe that you're not judging him. Your responsibility is to collect statements and evidence, the facts. After you've completed your investigation, you'll present your case to a magistrate. If the probable cause exists, warrants will be issued. It's important that the suspect understands that you're just the middleman.

Salespeople use the tactic of being the *middleman* all the time. They'll need to talk with the manager. The manager may have to talk with his supervisor. That salesperson may tell you that if it was up to him, he would do *this and that*, but it's that other guy who's preventing him. He's making you believe that he's trying to work with you (he wants what you want; it's the two of you, together) and any inability to fully satisfy your needs and/or wants is because of someone else, not him.

The salesman is never, really, the bad guy. Wink. Wink. Nudge. Nudge.

As I'm fond of saying, *I'm just trying to put pieces of a puzzle together; I'm not here to judge and I need your help putting this puzzle together.* So, put that *holier than thou attitude* away. Rest assured, I hate people who rape children, but when I interview those offenders, I leave my opinions at home with that cold beer waiting for me in the refrigerator.

Start the interview by introducing yourself; your introduction can be handled a couple of different ways. You can enter the interview with your chest puffed out and say, *I'm Investigator Paul McCormick with the Augusta County Sheriff's Office, and I'm investigating the rape of Jane Smith.* Or, and what I would recommend, *Hi, I'm Paul, an investigator with the Sheriff's Office. I appreciate you taking the time to talk with me. I'm sorry for this inconvenience.*

Then, ask the person about himself. Remember everyone's favorite topic of conversation? Me. We all love *me.* Where do you work? Hobbies? Family? Where were you born? Date of birth? Social Security number?

Ask for information he's unlikely to lie about, information you already know the answer to. Observe how he answers your questions while he's telling the truth. You can't compare apples to oranges if you don't know which one is which to begin with.

Questions/Discussion Points

Discuss baseline behavior. Can you obtain a baseline if you are accusatory in nature from the beginning of your contact with the accused? Why not?

Chapter 13
Guilty people know they are guilty— innocent people know they are innocent

I rarely call a person to arrange an interview; however, on those occasions when I do, I can learn something important. After asking him to come to the Sheriff's Office and he's agreed without asking why, I'll quickly put him on the top of the list as a likely suspect. The guilty person knows why I want to talk with him and usually won't ask because of his knowledge. The innocent person doesn't know why (he has no knowledge of the crime/the allegation against him) and will ask why I want to talk with him. He's an innocent man, answering his phone, with a cop asking him to come to the police station. He'll be thrown off and have honest and innocent questions: What's this about? What the hell is going on?

Remember, nothing is absolute, but it's worth noting.

So, I keep the introduction professional but minimize my air of absolute authority. I want to appear more human than just a cop on a mission. Law enforcement has a reputation for being cold, callous, and manipulative. The news media loves to focus on the bad ones, the corrupt ones, and the cops who have made poor decisions. Hollywood further reinforces that negative image by portraying us as being brutal and unethical. It makes for good movies; I love *Dirty Harry*. I become damn near giddy thinking about that movie.

Just like in any profession, there are good employees and bad ones.

Wall Street's reputation is in shambles right now (as I write this book). It has been before; it will be again; it's an easy target. Not every Wall Street trader is corrupt; however, the actions of a few have tarnished the reputation of many. So, the suspect has a valid perception of who you are and what you represent. That perception about you may not be correct, but you'll have greater success talking with someone if you accept what he believes is true (at least to him) until he has reason to believe otherwise.

Questions/Discussion Points

Discuss why people have a valid reason for distrusting law enforcement.

Chapter 14
Deviate from the script

Remember, during an interview you want the suspect to do most of the talking. You can take notes, but I recommend that you keep them to a minimum. If you start writing, it'll alert the suspect that you have found something noteworthy. There's a game afoot: you're paying attention to him; he's paying attention to you. He's trying to learn about you and what you know just as much as you are trying to do the same with him.

By talking with the suspect about everything except why he's there, you're not only establishing a baseline of behavior and speech, you're throwing him off. If guilty, he came with a script. He's prepared his story and wants to tell it, and you aren't allowing him. Because I used the word *script*, I should mention that if someone's account of events goes smoothly from point A to point Z without the occasional back and forth in the timeline, you should become suspicious.

> *We rarely tell a truthful story without occasionally backtracking because we inadvertently forgot some major detail.*

If a suspect's story/alibi does go smoothly (like a rehearsed script), he may be lying to you.

Questions/Discussion Points

Discuss a serious lie you have told.
How did you prepare for telling that lie?

Chapter 15
No one indicator of deception is an absolute determination of deception

Don't rest your decision of guilt on one moment of perceived deception.

On 11/18/11, I was watching the *Dr. Phil Show* (an embarrassing admission), with my 10-year-old son, during which Mike McQueary was being interviewed about the Jerry Sandusky situation (the assistant Penn State coach now convicted of child rape). McQueary was also an assistant coach who had witnessed one of the alleged rapes in a locker room shower. I noticed something exceedingly curious while he was being questioned by Dr. Phil. He closed his eyes for an extended period of time (at least 1.5 seconds), after being asked an especially intriguing question: *Did he, (McQueary), feel like he had done everything he could have done when he saw the abuse of that child in the shower?*

He, finally, answered, *Yes.*

I hollered *liar.*

My son asked why I declared him a *liar.* I explained what I had observed: McQueary had closed his eyes because he was attempting to hide, not face (look at), the person to who he was responding. 20/20 hindsight is brutal. The fact is: he did report the incident to Penn State officials. Years later, he became the focal point of national interest. From personal experience, I know that being in the media is damn near a lose/lose situation; not because of the media itself (not necessarily), it's the responses to the articles, the video postings. Everyone has an opinion.

Regardless, from that moment on, every time McQueary closed his eyes for a millisecond during the remainder of the interview, my son cried out, *"He's lying."*

That extended eye closure was something I hadn't observed before and the timeliness of it with Dr. Phil's question was note-worthy; however, it could've been an anomaly. So, I told my son that I was wrong for declaring McQueary a liar based on that one indicator.

Questions/Discussion Points

Why are absolutes dangerous?

Chapter 16
The man in the mirror is you, even if he ain't

One way to affect a change in the suspect's body *language* is to **mirror** him. One way to get someone more comfortable with you is to *mirror* him. A way to elicit truth is to make someone psychologically comfortable.

If his arms are crossed, you should do the same. If he uncrosses his arms then crosses his legs, you should do the same but not immediately; that would be too obvious. Eventually, you should adjust your body positioning and note whether or not he mirrors you. Once he mirrors you, he's subconsciously indicated a rapport.

It takes practice but attempt to mirror the individual you're interviewing. If he runs his hands through his hair, you should do the same, discretely. I'm bald, but I'll run my fingers across my scalp and scratch. If he leans forward, I'll lean forward. At some point, you should initiate the movements and observe if the individual begins to mirror you. If he does, you have begun the subconscious stage of rapport building. Use that power wisely: once he has started mirroring you, keep your body open. If you start crossing your arms and legs, he'll do the same which provides him with the barriers that you don't want him to have.

Watch people in public, in restaurants, anywhere people interact. You'll observe what I'm describing. You can practice at home with friends and family. Once you become aware of people and the power of body language, it opens a fascinating world of human interaction. People who're comfortable with each other tend to have open body positioning.

The basics are just that, basic. If he has his arms or legs crossed, he's created a barrier between you and him. In other words, you haven't established a rapport, and this wouldn't be the time to address the criminal matter.

We spread our legs and arms to define our space (our comfort zone). Men do it more than women. Women are more likely to cross their legs and arms to define their space.

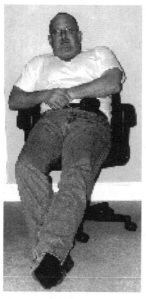 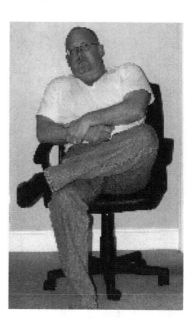

Barriers

Questions/Discussion Points

Watch and discuss people's behavior in public versus a social setting.

Chapter 17
Protecting the family jewels ...

There's more to language/communication than the definition of the actual words spoken. Words aren't needed to convey a message. I always see different statistics, but I'm comfortable in stating that approximately **85** percent of human communication falls outside the definition of the words spoken; it involves body language and one's voice—the tone, pitch, rate, and volume.

For example, think about dogs: one dog may roll onto its back and expose its throat to show submission to another dog. No vocalizations were necessarily needed. The message was clear.

One can observe the same type of submissive behavior in people. Someone, who feels inferior to another, may lower his head to avoid eye contact while bringing his shoulders inward and down, and/or the volume of his voice may be lower than his typical volume. He doesn't need to articulate that he feels threatened or inferior, his body and voice demonstrate it.

The likelihood that you, in response to being accused of doing something wrong, turning frontally to the accuser with your arms down by your side is unlikely. You'll blade off (partially turn away) to subconsciously protect your vital organs from the accuser.

Bladed off/Protecting Genitals

For some humor: if a man is being scolded by a woman, watch to see if he does something that provides a barrier between the woman and his genitals, like cupping his hands in front of his crotch. Odds are, he will.

Questions/Discussion Points

Practice saying hello and good-bye to each other. Alter these simple exchanges using tone of voice to make them threatening.

Chapter 18
I ran into the wall when you said what you said, because I'm desperate.

I've learned to pay a lot of attention to the suspect's legs and feet. Obviously, I'm not a neurologist, but I can see that the head (the brain) is further from the feet than the hands. We're more conscious of our hand movements because (I would argue rather simplistically), they (the hands and arms) are in our visual field; we use our hands to touch and feel; we use them more than our feet to consciously manipulate our environment. So, we are more careful about how our hands move when under stress.

Most people have been exposed to some level of the science of detecting deception. There are books and television shows on it. People have learned that they'll cover their eyes (to avoid looking at the person they are lying to) or mouth (to *hide* the lie) when they lie. They'll fidget with their fingers (an action that distracts the liar from fully engaging with the person being lied to). They'll pick at unseen lint, a grooming gesture (an action that helps calm the liar and also disengages him from the one being lied to). With that knowledge, they'll attempt to avoid those behaviors. But their feet are so far removed from their thought process (having so much more to worry about: *What words to use? What story am I telling? What am I doing with my hands? What am I doing with my eyes?*), they'll tend to forget about them.

Let's assume the exit door to the interrogation room is off to the suspect's right. Now, you ask him a question regarding the crime and his feet or foot suddenly point off to the right (toward the door), he's subconsciously looking for the exit because he wants out; he's scared.

If he starts tapping his foot or his hands start tapping his leg, when asked an accusatory question, he's trying to deal with that rush of adrenalin released by his autonomic nervous system.

Simply put, he has nervous energy.

A person fidgets because he doesn't know how to deal with the physiological reactions to the psychological threats.

> **Accusatory questions are threatening.**

Grooming

Hiding a Lie

Questions/Discussion Points

Watch a political debate. What nervous/deceptive behaviors can you observe?

Chapter 19
Whatchya lookin' at, Dude?

I'll re-emphasize that the detection of deception is about clusters of behavior. In the scientific world, the word is *validation*. Is what you observed repeatable? Or, was it just an artifact, an anomaly? Is what you're observing truly a sign of deception?

It's also important to note that you should have some knowledge of the culture in which the suspect was raised. There's too much emphasis (in the United States) on *the suspect didn't look at me when answering a question; so, he must be lying.* But, if he was raised in the Asian culture, he was showing you respect: you don't look an authority figure in the eye; that act is disrespectful.

What you know isn't necessarily what the suspect knows; cultures are distinct and different.

Questions/Discussion Points

Discuss cultural differences: poor vs rich, urban vs suburban, not necessarily eastern vs western.

Chapter 20
The closer you are, the more screwed up I feel

There are physical stages of social interaction that involve personal space and levels of personal comfort defined by that physical space between two people. Edward T. Hall (an anthropologist) introduced the concept of *proxemics*. For the most part, *intimate space* is within a range of two feet, whispering and touching that comes from a comfortable knowledge of and security with a person, family member, or lover; *personal space* is two feet to four feet, or a close friend; *social space* is four feet to ten feet and involves acquaintances, coworkers, and people you are familiar with on a daily basis; *public space* is ten feet and beyond or strangers.

Those distances may vary: if someone is standing behind me, the distances needed for my comfort will increase. If someone is standing four feet in front of me, a person I'm somewhat familiar with, my stress level will be relatively low. However, if that same person is standing four feet **behind** me, my stress level will be higher. In other words, it becomes somewhat about the visual field. My wife can stand directly behind me, and that's fine. If a best friend is standing directly behind me, I will have a completely different physiological response to him than my wife. Many of my law enforcement friends have played horrible tricks on me. My wife hasn't been as cruel. So those spaces vary depending on visual fields and circumstances.

The easiest way to intrude on someone's *intimate space* is to shake hands with him. While shaking hands, you can place your other hand on the person's elbow. Not only does that action provide you with some physical control (if it becomes necessary) that hand on the elbow also sends a subconscious message to the other person: he's not in control, you are; you're the dominate one.

When you shake hands with someone, if you want to demonstrate dominance, you want the webbing in between the thumb and index finger of your hand to meet with the webbing of the other person's hand. Now subtly (as you begin to apply your handshake grip) rotate your hand so that your palm angles toward the ground, just a slight angle not to exceed five degrees. You want your grip to be firm but not exceeding the other person's grip (respect). If you are overly aggressive, the other person will respond and you will be in a power struggle. If done properly, your hand will discretely exhibit physical authority over the person whose hand you're shaking.

Never underestimate the importance of a handshake.

Questions/Discussion Points

Discuss your experiences with handshakes: the sweaty palm, the vice grip, the limp hand.

Chapter 21
No isn't necessarily no, when I've given you a ride home

In November 2011, Deputy Don Moran and I investigated allegations of aggravated sexual battery. The victim was 17-years-old, and the suspect, David Garner, was a 24-year-old coworker. She'd reported that, when Garner gave her a ride home, he pulled into a vacant parking lot. She agreed (although somewhat reluctantly) to making out, to kissing. He, according to her written statement, forcibly groped her breasts and rubbed her vaginal area over her pants; she also reported that he lifted up her shirt and bra and licked her breasts, despite her repeated statements to stop. He physically got on top of her (*pinned her*); he'd forced himself upon her. He'd allegedly told her that she owed him for the ride home.

Deputy Moran had discovered, during his research, that a Jane Smith had previously filed a sexual assault complaint against Garner (when he was a juvenile), and he'd pled that the facts were sufficient for a prosecution and the matter was taken under advisement for 12 months; furthermore, Moran also knew of another report filed against Garner for something (amazingly enough) similar to a sexual assault that was not prosecuted because the victim had not wanted to pursue the matter.

So, we went to Garner's house, where he lived with his parents. He and his parents met us outside, and we introduced ourselves. I asked a relatively simple question of Garner: had he given Annette a ride home the other night? In response, he became closed off; he crossed his arms and avoided eye contact, when before he had not. He finally answered that he had, indeed, given her a ride. Instead of delving into the allegations, I asked him about his relationship with the accuser; I asked him about his place of employment.

We talked. I continued to get a sense of how he responded to relatively nonthreatening questions. His eye contact resumed. He physically opened up again.

However, he was still eager to address the issue at hand: *why were we there?* His parents were trying to intervene. I advised them that their son was an adult, and we would like to speak with him privately. The father grumbled something about their son being an adult and having to handle his own problems and he started to walk off; the mother stated something to the effect of not liking it, but she too walked off, toward the house.

Their son stayed with me. Immediately, based on his parents' response, I assumed they knew why we were there. If parents walk away from their child, adult or juvenile, you should consider that a clue. If any known loved one walks away from a suspect, while you're questioning him, it's noteworthy. Body language goes beyond just observing the suspect. How do those around the suspect react? The parents, in this case, were distancing themselves from someone they loved; they weren't protecting him anymore.

David's parents were fed up with defending their son. They knew what he had done. I'm sure of it.

David Garner had been accused twice before of being overly aggressive with women. Remember that bitch of an id? *I want what I want when I want it;* sex is a strong motivator. Remember being a teenager, the hormones? I'm by no means excusing his behavior. It's just a matter of perspective.

We all tend to forget that we weren't as *rational* then as we are now. And the words *then (past), now (present),* and *rational (the power of reason)* are very subjective terms subject to future interpretation and alteration. How many of our memories are truly accurate, factual accounts of what actually occurred (at the time)? Memories are constantly modified by ongoing life experience.

We tend to minimize our previous bad behaviors and exaggerate our good behaviors.

The interview continued: *Describe Annette to me. What's she like? How long have you known each other? How would you describe her as a person?*

They'd known each other for a couple years through work. He described their relationship as platonic. They'd never kissed. She'd confide in him about her relationship problems.

I asked him if Annette was a liar and he responded that she wasn't.

Asking someone if the accuser is a liar is one of my favorite questions to ask to make some determination of guilt. An innocent person will usually declare the accuser a liar; he won't hesitate, if the accuser is lying. If you didn't do the crime and someone has falsely accused you of doing it, what's the simple response? *Yes, the accuser is a liar:* **yes**. The guilty will usually make some comment like: *I wouldn't call him a liar, he must be mistaken; he's just got it wrong.* The accused may hem and haw before making some weak statement about the accuser being a liar. The guilty very rarely, and with timeliness in their response, say, *Yes, the accuser is a liar.* Again, nothing is absolute. No **one** thing should lead you to decry deception. It's about those clusters of behavior and responses. But, I must admit, I love that question.

During my interview of David Garner, I kept my body open, and I stayed within four feet of him, within his personal space. I briefly mirrored him with partially closed arms; however, for the most part, I kept my hands and arms open. Slowly, he did the same; he lowered his arms.

After further conversation, I sat on the lawn, alongside his driveway. Garner had been clutching his pack of cigarettes; I'm a smoker and lit up my cigarette. He unclenched his hands; he relaxed and joined me. A nonsmoker could have just as easily given him permission to smoke.

He didn't sit on the driveway but squatted in front of me, with full frontal positioning. His crotch was exposed. It's primal, but it's something to be aware of. When someone exposes parts of their body that are vulnerable (genitals, chest, heart, and lungs), he's subconsciously communicated a level of comfort/trust with you. You've established a rapport.

Deputy Moran stayed off to the side, but he, too, squatted. He kept an eye on the parents who had retreated into their home. Moran didn't intrude into the suspect's visual field; he remained nonthreatening but was ready to respond if a response was necessary. He allowed the suspect to stay focused on me.

Before Deputy Moran and I left, the suspect had confirmed everything in the victim's written statement. He'd even admitted to remembering that the victim had said *she can't* at least once. The whole encounter took less than 40 minutes. Recently, he pled guilty to a misdemeanor sexual battery charge. The victim didn't want to testify. She was being pressured by her friends; she just misunderstood. Garner was a good guy.

Questions/Discussion Points

Discuss ways to deal with family and friends of the suspect because they may be present during your initial contact.

Chapter 22
Words spoken —
I live with my lies

Victims make false allegations.

Like it or not, *people* file false police reports.

It happens all the **damn** time.

In 2006, I testified against a woman who had reported that she'd been abducted and raped. Her case had quickly become a multi-jurisdictional issue involving three agencies. She reported being abducted at gunpoint by a pregnant woman and a man in the City of Staunton; she was raped in Augusta County, as the pregnant woman watched. She also indicated that she thought the incident was related to her having to testify in court against someone scheduled for an upcoming Waynesboro City Circuit Court case—witness intimidation.

I was tasked (along with others) with investigating that rape, abduction, and witness intimidation. With three agencies involved, there were over 60 man-hours dedicated to this case in approximately 36 hours.

Ultimately, she (the nonvictim victim) was convicted of filing a false report. It's not a popular opinion in today's world of sensitivity and political correctness, but people do file false reports (all too often) for violent crime (including rape). She'd alleged three felonies and was convicted only of filing one false report (a misdemeanor) and received community service.

An allegation is just that, an allegation, until probable cause elevates that allegation into a criminal proceeding.

I have no problem telling a suspect that the allegation against him may be false; it may be bullshit. False allegations happen; people do lie, but I won't know until we talk. Sometimes, those words (*It's bullshit; it may be a malicious lie*) are the words that may physically open up a person's body and his psychological barriers because I've indicated that I'm open to hearing his version of events.

Letting the suspect know that a truth (an allegation) can be tainted with lies (exaggerations) may open passages of dialogue.

Lies originate from truth. Truth is tainted with inaccuracy. Lies are tainted with truth. Explore them.

Questions/Discussion Points

Discuss how you would approach a victim about him filing a false report. Everyone has a motive.

Chapter 23
Apologies are wonderful confessions

The suspect is expecting you to come out swinging, accusing him of his guilt. When you don't, it throws him off.

Depending on how things are going in the interrogation, it might be worth pointing out your observations (his vulnerabilities), but it's about how you approach them. If you confront him with *I clearly see that you are lying because you do **this or that***, you'll risk him saying, *screw you* **or** *I'm out of here*. However, if you approach him with: *I can see that you're upset; you're angry; you're a good person who's struggling because I can see it in your eyes. (It's hard to be where you're at, in this investigation; I understand),* he's more likely to continue talking.

Don't specifically point out what you are seeing, just that you're experiencing from him some form of **remorse / conscience**, (anything the suspect may find redeeming). *Conscience* and *remorse (because he's a decent person)* can be good escape words for a person caught in a lie. When all else fails, a person can wrap himself up within his *guilt*: **I'm so sorry for** ... and he'll minimize. (Rest assured, he will minimize.)

However, as long as he's apologizing for elements of the crime, he's confessing. Let him apologize.

Questions/Discussion Points

Discuss the importance of developing rapport and how that rapport can allow for an apology/confession. Remember, no one likes to be judged.

Chapter 24
I spy with my eye ...

Our brain is divided into two sides called lobes. The right side is more artistically/emotionally oriented; the left side is more logically oriented. Our nervous system is wired backward because of the *corpus callosum*, which connects the left and right hemispheres of our brain. On average, a physically right-side-dominate person (a person who writes with his right hand) is left-brain-dominate, or logical; a person who writes with his left hand is right-brain-dominate, or creative/emotional.

Neuro-Linguistic Programming was developed by John Grinder (assistant professor of linguistics at the University of California, Santa Cruz) and Richard Bandler (student of psychotherapy) in the 1970s. There's been controversy over some of their concepts; however, I will share with you what I have seen in my personal experience. It should be noted: Neuro-Linguistic Programming was never intended to be used for the detection of deception. But, it's often referred to as a means for detecting deception. I can't emphasize enough in this book: every person is different; techniques are techniques, and they won't apply to everyone.

> *An interrogator must be fluid and adapt to each individual.*

Based on Grinder and Bandler's research, if a person's eyes look upward when he's asked a question, he's a visual person or a visual recaller. If he's an auditory person, he'll look to the side, toward his ears. An emotional recaller will look down. In keeping with that, if you ask someone a question *requiring* him to recall visual information, he'll look upward. If you ask him what he heard, he'll look toward his ears. If you ask someone how he felt about something, he'll look down.

Back to brain dominance: A person will look off to either the right or left side. I rarely see a person roll his eyes straight up or straight down, when answering a question. My experience has shown me that a left-brain-dominate person typically looks toward the right and visa versa. I will not state whether or not certain eye movement is an indication of deception. That's a mess of conflicting information. To keep it simple, we're creatures of habit. I typically cross my right leg over my left and my left arm over my right because that's what feels most comfortable. It's no different with the eyes. We have established patterns.

Grinder and Bandler furthered offered that the auditory, visual, or emotional recaller could also be detected through the words he uses. The visual recaller will make statements like *I can* **picture** *that* or *I **see** what you are saying*. I have difficulty saying words like *hear* (I can **hear** *that*; that **sounds** about right) when interviewing an auditory person because I'm a visual person. I especially have trouble with emotional people and saying such phrases as *it **feels** like* and *it's **painful** to say*.

Try to further connect (establish a rapport) with a person by using the words he uses. Again, we like people who are like us. Musicians hang out with musicians; they talk music (meter, notes, chords, progressions). Law enforcement hangs out with law enforcement; we talk cop stuff (the law, war stories, frustration).

**People who are similar to us
speak our language.**

When interviewing someone, I'll watch his eyes when asking known truth questions and (sometimes) I'll make a note of his eye pattern with an arrow on my note paper. It can be confusing, and that simple documentation keeps it relatively simple. However, to break it down into deception: Once you've established the suspect's typical eye behavior, if the suspect's eyes deviate from that norm (when asked an accusatory question, after a baseline has been established), you may want to consider revisiting the question that elicited that deviation in eye behavior—maybe.

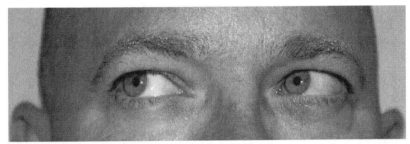

Visual recaller (I see what you're saying)

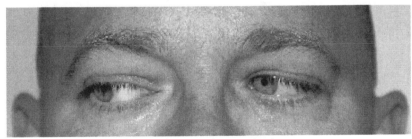

Auditory recaller (I hear what you're saying)

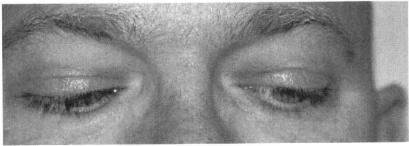

Emotional recaller (It feels like)

I don't put too much emphasis on eye behavior. It's more of an ongoing curiosity because there's so much debate about it: left or right, up or down, internal dialogue vs. emotional recall, recall vs. construct, deception or no deception. Eyelid behavior is more telling (in my opinion); it's a more reliable indicator of deception: that is, eye closure to avoid eye contact; increased eyelid blinking, when asked a threatening question, which is a reaction to the pupils having dilated and that momentary discomfort caused by the increased amount of light entering the eye.

Regardless, a deviation in eye behavior can include the suspect looking directly into your eyes. If he hasn't demonstrated direct eye contact during most of your questioning and suddenly engages you in direct eye contact during certain questions, he may be attempting to disguise his lie with the American belief that eye contact is *always* a sign of truthfulness, or he's challenging you. Certainly, it could be a sign of truthfulness; however, the detection of deception is about the suspect's deviations from his established norm, his baseline.

Are you comparing apples to oranges or fruit to vegetables? Without a baseline, you'll never know.

Nothing is absolute. There are no hard and fast rules for positively identifying (100 percent of the time) deception.

Questions/Discussion Points

Discuss language within different professions.
Discuss how you would adapt to a person's language.

Chapter 25
Empathy can be a powerful tool

How you physically approach and present yourself to a person can make or break your interview/interrogation before you have uttered the first word.

Usually, I'm professionally dressed: dress slacks, a button down shirt, and a tie. I rarely wear my suit jacket during an interview, and I certainly don't have my sidearm or any other weapon in the interrogation room. I'm already displaying my badge of authority. There's no need to further rub the suspect's nose in it. Certainly, if you're wearing your department issued uniform, all the clues for him to know that you're a police officer are on display.

How you approach witnesses is crucial as well. Witnesses can be reluctant to reveal the truth; they can be just as deceptive as the suspect. Family and friends will lie to protect those people who they love or care for.

Remember, *everyone is capable of lying*. On a daily basis, everyone lies during normal social interaction.

I recall a case from 2010. The defendant, Daryl Davis, was facing abduction with a gun; he'd held his girlfriend, O'Creene, captive for two hours and had choked her. When she came to my office to report the incident, she had bruising around her neck. I took her information and Investigator Brian Jenkins photographed her injuries. I don't usually do this, but (based on the physical evidence and her written statement and my analysis of it), I immediately obtained warrants for her boyfriend's arrest.

Investigator Jenkins had Davis in custody within 60 minutes, but Davis invoked Miranda. In order to further investigate my case, I went to his parents' residence, where he resided in their finished basement. That's where the incident allegedly occurred. With my digital recorder recording, I introduced myself to his parents. I asked if I could speak with them. They already knew that their son was being held without bond. I offered my apologies for having to meet under these circumstances. We sat in their living room while speaking about their son's relationship with the victim. I implied that she was a difficult person to deal with, and Davis's parents' confirmed that their son had recently separated from her and was having a difficult time with it. I asked if they had routine access to his living space, and they stated that they did.

I asked if they would allow me to photograph it, and they agreed.

I also asked if their son owned a gun. The father explained that his son didn't, but there was a nonoperative air pistol in the basement, owned by the father.

I went to the basement, with their consent, and reminded them that they didn't have to cooperate with me; however, I was just trying to be thorough because I wanted to obtain the truth about what had occurred that afternoon in their house.

The mother told me that her son had admitted to choking his ex-girlfriend, O'Creene. That was recorded. That was evidence.

I located the air pistol where the victim said it would be located; I photographed it and the basement; the father allowed me to collect the pistol as evidence. I was *genuinely* apologetic (every step of the way) for what they must have been going through. When leaving their home, I thanked them for their cooperation. I offered my condolences. After all, he was their son; they loved him.

Now, several months later, I'm on the witness stand during the preliminary hearing. All my recordings had been made available to the defense. The assistant commonwealth's attorney and I had anticipated that the defense would attempt to attack my search of the defendant's room. That wasn't a real issue, just a nuisance in court; however, it's the responsibility of the defense to argue those finer points of the law: Did the suspect's parents have that legal authority to grant me permission for the search? However, the defense attorney surprised me instead with: *You told my client's mother that her son had confessed* to the allegations, which wasn't true. I'll admit that I hesitated for a moment; I wasn't prepared for that accusation.

I'll assume that the defense attorney hadn't listened to my recording; he'd relied solely on the mother's account of what I had allegedly said and done. Frankly, it would have been neither here nor there if I had, indeed, lied to the mother, but I was able to shut down what may have been the defense's attempt at attacking my integrity.

After an uncomfortably lengthy pause, I replied with: *No I didn't. Your client invoked Miranda. I wouldn't have lied to his mother.* There weren't any more questions; that was the end of my testimony. I'll guess the defense, after that preliminary hearing, finally listened to the audio and realized I'd been completely honest with the parents. I **had confirmed** their domain over their son's room; I'd provided them with the opportunity to **not** cooperate with my investigation. Furthermore, I **had not** lied to them.

Davis's parents were in crisis, and I used empathy (and their state of crisis) to obtain what I needed for my case. Had I been cold and indifferent (had I stated that their son was *an ass* for what he had done), I doubt that my visit in their home would have resulted in the collection of the gun (without a search warrant), photographs of the crime scene (without a search warrant), and a recording of his mother acknowledging her son's confession to her.

During their crisis, I provided them with some sense of order; I was answering questions and providing comfort (empathy) while collecting evidence. My actions were calculated, on a variety of levels, but genuine: I *cared* about the victim; I *cared* about the suspect's parents; I *cared* about the **truth**. Somewhere, within all that (the events of that afternoon), there had been an offender. Probable cause is about the preponderance of truth. The suspect screwed up. Like it or not, he committed a crime (a couple serious felonies).

Months later, Davis's parents wanted to protect him. Their memory of my conduct had deviated from what had actually occurred between us. I don't believe that Davis's mother purposefully lied to the defense attorney. Her memory could have easily been affected by motive. Her son was facing prison, and she could have been, understandably, motivated to protect him from that possibility and determined to protect him. I believe that her memory of that evening (months earlier/the past) had been tainted by what I was representing to her (now/the present): the man who could separate her from her son. I'm not naïve though; she may have blatantly lied to Davis's attorney about my conduct.

Within some sense of abstraction, the past, present, and future can be documented on a digital recorder. Don't underestimate it, a recording.

Regardless, Davis's case was certified, and he recently accepted a plea deal of three years in prison; although the victim wasn't overly eager to prosecute him. The last I'd heard was that the victim and her family were upset with me because they only wanted him to receive counseling for his *anger issues*. Sometimes that happens: the victim comes to you wanting help; you do your job and later the victim makes you into the bad guy. It's very common in domestic situations.

Questions/Discussion Points

Discuss empathy and how it can be successfully used to obtain information.

Can you be genuinely empathic with the person and still elicit information?

Chapter 26
Defense attorneys are no different than prosecutors. They are about obtaining the truth.

The evidence of my conduct can become part of the permanent record whenever it's needed. It doesn't take long for defense attorneys to get to know you, and you'll get to know them. I'm actually friendly with most; I respect them and their responsibilities; we're all tasked with the same responsibility: truth. No one wants an innocent man to go to prison. Whether or not a defense attorney personally likes me is not a real concern; my main priority is to be recognized as honest. If he has an issue with me and how I've conducted an interview/interrogation, a recording is available for review in court. I've yet to have a confession tossed out of evidence.

There've been some legal debates about the admissibility of my interrogations, but a judge or jury has always been afforded the opportunity to hear every word spoken by me and every word spoken by the accused. In court, my past cases and investigations have provided me with a lot of credibility. You can't buy that. You earn it, and I sincerely believe that a recorded documentation of what you've said during an interview and/or interrogation goes a long way in establishing that credibility.

I have nothing to hide.

Questions/Discussion Points

Do you have any physical or verbal mannerisms that can be negatively perceived?

Chapter 27
Sometimes a box is more than a box

You want to control the interrogation environment as much as possible by minimizing distractions. The accepted standard for an interrogation room is a 10-foot by 10-foot room without windows, clocks, or anything on the walls. There should be two chairs: one for the suspect and one for the interrogator. The suspect's chair shouldn't have wheels, making him reasonably immobile. The interrogator's chair should have wheels. The interrogator should sit slightly higher than the suspect. That's it. There should be nothing else in that room, nowhere for the suspect to hide, like behind a table. You want him fully exposed.

Carolina Blue is considered a good color for the interrogation room; my polygraph room is painted that color. It's considered psychologically authoritative to the suspect while simultaneously calming him.

You want the room set up for audio/visual recording. Sometimes you miss indicators of deception the first time around; most importantly though—as previously mentioned—recordings take a lot of fight out of an attorney's defense. A court case can take months (upward to years) before it's presented to a judge or jury. A recording minimizes the defense's ability to introduce doubt about the content of your report. If you record everything, the defense can't say that you threatened his client or you badgered him until he confessed or that you misquoted him in your report. The list goes on, but that's the defense's job: to keep law enforcement honest and to create reasonable doubt.

Written transcripts aren't *perfect* because they are subject to the transcriptionist's interpretation of the recording. Memories aren't perfect.

Recordings allow for everyone to make their own assessment.

It's wonderful to have an interrogation played for a jury in which you were respectful, calm, and patient with the suspect.

I'll admit though, I had a recording hurt me in court. A grandfather, Raider (in a case I had to investigate), admitted to *accidentally* touching his granddaughter's breasts multiple times over the summer of 2010. His granddaughter had disclosed that he had groped her breasts; he had "raped" her. Her definition of *rape*, obtained during a forensic interview, was: *he had molested her, touched her.*

I was gentle. I was calm with Raider during his interrogation, in his home; however, as my interrogation was played (as the jury listened), I knew I was in trouble and the case was in trouble.

I sat on the stand and spiraled into a personal hell.

I became argumentative with the defense attorney. I became defensive. After the trial, a bailiff told me that he'd never seen me that way on the stand. I had allowed the defense attorney to get under my skin. Furthermore, I came across (to the judge and jury) as being arrogant. Arrogance is ugly.

> *Never argue with a defense attorney.*
> *Just answer his questions.*
> *Answer them simply.*

The defendant was sitting with his defense attorney. Raider was 65 years old, frail, and pathetic; he had to constantly leave the courtroom to urinate because of the medication he was on, and he was bent over as if he was in pain. He wasn't that way a year earlier; when I saw him, he was very mobile and lucid. Regardless, he was what one envisions as the stereotype of the elderly: kindly, sweet, and innocent. It's hard to imagine a grandparent committing a felony, especially if he's suffering from an assortment of physical ailments. Our instinct is to care for and coddle the sick and elderly.

I'm bald and 225 pounds, and I sounded like some manipulative/coercive cop; that stereotype was there. I made it easy for the jury to distrust me, especially because I had become argumentative with the defense attorney and had appeared big and uncaring—a cop with an agenda.

During my interrogation a year earlier, Raider easily accepted the possibility that he may have *accidentally* touched his granddaughter's breasts at least twelve times over three months. I overly stressed the numbers, and one could argue that Raider was confused by my questions. His defense attorney certainly did.

The interrogation lasted less than 45 minutes, but the damage was done. I saw the jury look at me in an unfavorable way.

If Raider had *looked* like some stereotypical criminal, I doubt that my techniques would have sounded manipulative to the jury. I was merely minimizing the allegations: When massaging someone's shoulders from behind, my experience has been that *accidentally* touching the breasts was more of an intentional action, on my part, in hopes of arousing my adult female partner. That was my thought process. I just figured the more I could get Raider to talk about *accidentally* touching his granddaughter's breast, the worse he would sound to a judge or jury in the future.

Twelve times, in my opinion, was less of an *accident* and more of a pattern of purposeful behavior.

Despite the fact that Raider later admitted to the jury (he actually testified on the stand) to buying and giving his granddaughter a vibrator, he was found **not** guilty, in less than 15 minutes, of aggravated sexual battery.

I failed; my testimony failed; my interrogation failed.

Now, when it comes to the elderly, I'm exceptionally careful with how I interrogate them. I'm exceedingly mindful of how the elderly suspect will appear to the jury, of how I'll appear to the jury in juxtaposition to the elderly suspect.

To keep it all in perspective: my situation with Raider was really no different than any other case. A suspect always looks different in court: clean, well-kept hair; formally dressed; sober; the list goes on. He certainly looks different than when he was arrested. I certainly look different on a Saturday night, when I'm unshaven and wearing my well-worn jeans and favorite torn and stained white t-shirt with a beer in hand, than I do when I'm professionally dressed for work on Monday.

Stereotypes.

Questions/Discussion Points

Discuss how physical appearance can and does influence a person's perception of guilt or innocence. Like it or not, it happens.

Chapter 28
When the clock starts ticking, I'm on the run

The bulk of my caseload involves child sex crimes. When dealing with child victims, a confession from the offender is vital in successfully prosecuting the case. Children are not generally good witnesses. A seven-year-old on the stand testifying about how Uncle Bob stuck his *pee-pee* into her *monkey* is rarely enough for a guilty verdict. I can't blame a jury for being hesitant to put a man in prison for 20 years for raping a child when the victim (age seven) is talking about *pee-pees*, *monkeys*, and *milk*. There are no witnesses and there's rarely any physical evidence. It's just a sweet young girl (or boy), with no motive to lie, testifying from the witness stand (in a very intimidating room) with the offender looking right at her or him. The accused is always an *upstanding citizen of the community*, who'll have a list of character witnesses attesting to that.

Once a child has disclosed sexual abuse, the clock is ticking. It doesn't take long for the accused to hear through the grapevine that he's been accused of molestation. Furthermore, it's hard for parents to accept that a relative (a brother or sister of the victim, a grandmother or grandfather, an aunt or uncle) committed the offense. There must be a mistake, a misunderstanding. The child becomes the focal point of the family. She's a liar. She saw it on television. Someone has put her up to it, especially if there's a custody dispute. I strive for a quick resolution because a confession validates the child's disclosure; that validation allows for more family members to fully support the child through his healing process.

The vast majority of sexual offenses against children are committed by someone the child knows: a trusted family friend or a dearly loved family member. The stranger molester is very rare.

I need a confession.

Questions/Discussion Points

Discuss the pressure of obtaining a confession and how to temper it in order to establish rapport.

Chapter 29
Home invasion

I could call my suspect and invite him to my office. When he gets there, I could walk him into the interrogation room and start the rapport building. However, I'll already have two strikes against me. That initial phone call has alerted him that the jig was up, and he'll start preparing his alibi. Second, when he walks into that interrogation room, his defenses are going to be on high alert. Hollywood may misrepresent the interrogation process, but everyone knows that things aren't going well if you're sitting in a sterile environment (the box) with a cop sitting across from you.

Most likely though, if I call the suspect to arrange a meeting, he may agree to it the day after tomorrow because he has some charity work he needs to tend to but, after he hangs up the phone, he'll have time to think (to think some more) and then he'll call me back to advise me that he'll be obtaining the services of an attorney.

So, contrary to accepted wisdom, I'll visit him at his residence and do my interview and interrogation on his turf, in his home. I've had great success in obtaining confessions that way. Remember our 24-year-old man, David Garner? His confession was obtained on his driveway, with his parents not so far away.

I won't approach a suspect at work.

I won't interrogate a gang member in his environment. I'm not oblivious to officer safety. The last time I confronted a gang member in his home was after I had a search warrant in hand and our Augusta County S.W.A.T. team had already secured the residence and had everyone's rapt attention (flash bangs and AR-15s have a way of getting someone's attention).

A lot of a person's identity is associated with his employment. If I unnecessarily threaten that, I'll be met with very hard obstacles to overcome. I'll wait until I know that he'll be home, and then I'll come knocking on his door.

> **Approaching someone at their place of employment for a confession, unless it's absolutely necessary, is a virtual guarantee for failure.**

I always have a cell phone with me, but I'll often leave my police radio in the car. I don't want that constant radio traffic reminding the suspect that I'm an investigator. I'll do my best to minimize any reminders that I'm a Sheriff's Deputy. If I do have my radio, I'll keep the volume as low as possible.

After the suspect has opened the door, I'll introduce myself using his formal name (respect). I'll explain that my name is *Paul, and I'm an Investigator with the Augusta County Sheriff's Office* (minimizing my authority). *I'm sorry to inconvenience you at this time. May I come in?* I've guided him into an affirmative response by being polite. We'll shake hands while I'm thanking him for his time (intimate space). Generally, people don't want to be rude when someone is nonthreatening and polite. More times than not, I'm invited into the home. It then becomes psychologically difficult for the suspect to kick me out.

Remember my reference to Maslow and the esteem stage of development? We want friendship; we want people to like us. The guilty are especially needy; the guilty really want you to like them, to believe them. Their ability to stay out of prison depends on you liking and believing them and their story.

A general rule of thumb: if you've been politely, but firmly, telling a suspect that you're having difficulty understanding his alibi (his denials) and he stays with you, the longer he does it (tolerating you as you systematically dismantle his story), the more likely it is that he's indeed guilty. Innocent people will only take so much before they lawyer up and/or tell you to exit their residence.

> *The guilty don't want you to leave until they believe that you believe them.*

Once I'm in the house, I'll take further but subtle control of the suspect and his environment. If a television or radio is on (and one or the other usually is), I'll ask the suspect to turn it off because I'm easily *distracted*, and noise makes it difficult for me to concentrate. I certainly don't tell him that the background noise diminishes the quality of my audio recording. The suspect always obliges. Then again, that's not always true. No sooner had I written that the suspect always obliges to turning off the television, I had one (no joke, the following day) say, "No." I was with Social Services, in a man's home, and I asked him if he could turn off his television; it was exceedingly loud. He looked at me and said that he wouldn't turn it off because the last time he did (at the request of a cop) he wound up saying something and being arrested. I laughed to myself. After a few minutes, when he was more comfortable with me, he (without being asked again) turned off the television.

Then, I'll ask for us to sit. He'll agree because it's customary for people to sit while having a conversation. I now have another decision to make: do I sit in his seat or do I allow him to sit in it? His seat is easily determined. Where are the remote controls for the television? Where are the newspapers and/or magazines? Which seat is more worn? By sitting in his seat, I've completely usurped his control over his environment. I usually do this only if

I've established that he has guns. If he does, he'll likely keep them handy. If I'm in his seat, the concealed gun is now likely near me, not him. More often than not, I'll allow the suspect to sit where he wants. Again, I want him to be comfortable. He's already threatened by my presence, and I want to decrease his discomfort.

If the suspect asks why I need to speak with him, I'll answer with a variation of: *Allegations have been made against you, and it's my job to investigate them. I know that people can lie or misunderstand things, but it's my job to uncover the truth. I'm sure you can appreciate that, can't you?* Invariably, he'll answer with a *Yes.* Now, this is where I can establish my first clue. The guilty rarely ask what the allegations are because they know why I'm sitting in front of them. If they do ask, they are easily redirected. They are willing to wait and learn what I know; they can be unusually patient. The innocent will usually ask for specifics right away: *What do you mean? Who accused me of what?*

> **The innocent are far less patient than the guilty. It's not set in stone, but it's something to pay attention for.**

If the suspect asks for specifics, I'll try to take the conversation elsewhere. If he's adamant, then I'll tell him, but I'll minimize the allegation by saying: *I'm sure it's much to do about nothing, a misunderstanding, but your niece has made some statements about you inappropriately touching her.* I won't say: *she said that you fingered her.*

To get that confession, you should initially approach the suspect as if he's innocent. Remember, let the suspect tell his account of events, his alibi. Furthermore, how would you want a family member treated? How would you want to be treated? I've interviewed a law enforcement officer who was accused of criminal offenses. I treated him with respect. Not because he was a cop, I dealt with him as a person. People respond well to respect.

You don't want to unnecessarily activate the suspect's autonomic nervous system. It's a game. Plain and simple: you're playing a game of chess that will later be reviewed by attorneys.

Questions/Discussion Points

Debate the use of the interrogation room vs the suspect's residence. There isn't a correct answer.

Chapter 30
I did what, with who?

Cognitive dissonance is a big term for being all screwed up psychologically. Cognitive dissonance is created when someone possesses two conflicting thoughts or ideas simultaneously. We strive to reduce stress and possessing conflicting ideas increases our stress. In keeping with the theme of this book, a person may know that telling the truth is morally correct because he was raised to tell the truth and has reaped some benefits for having told the truth in the past, but now telling the truth could land him in prison and prison is a scary place.

He wants to tell the truth, but he can't tell the truth.

The suspect wants to know what you know while trying to make you believe what he wants you to believe, his lies; however, you could also discover his lies that will send him off to prison. If he makes you leave, you may become suspicious.

He's off kilter; he's experiencing cognitive dissonance.

In 2007, I interviewed a 24-year-old woman, Sarah Reynolds in an interrogation room for having a sexual relationship with a 14-year-old boy. That boy had been reluctant to give up information because he loved her. The father of the 14-year-old boy knew about his son's relationship and started a similar relationship with Sarah. He threatened to turn her into the police, if she didn't.

Reynolds was stuck between that proverbial rock and a hard place. She loved the 14-year-old boy; she was being blackmailed by the boy's father; and I represented prison.

Reynolds met me at the Sheriff's Office; I observed that she was sad and scared. She was defeated. I took her into the interrogation room. It didn't take long to establish a rapport because I remained physically open and used a soothing voice. Again, there was nothing amazing about how I interacted with her. However, it's all too easy to be rushed and forget to slow down and genuinely engage the person you're interviewing.

I wasn't there to judge her; I repeatedly and reassuringly told her that. Quite frankly, based on her history, I had no doubt that she was an abused woman. Even though that 14-year-old boy was the victim in this case, I had also researched her as a victim— victimology. As a result of my research, I speculated that she desired the love and affection of someone who would not beat her, someone who would unconditionally love her.

When she started to cry, I slowly moved into her intimate space. I reassured her; I knew he loved her (and he did; he and I had talked at some length) and that she loved him. I acknowledged her past history of suspected physical abuse. She nodded and cried some more.

> *There was mucus. If you don't see or hear mucus, when someone is crying, that crying is probably fake.*

She fell into what is commonly referred to as the confession mode; she had gone from sitting somewhat upright into a slumped-over position; her head and shoulders were down toward her knees. When a suspect slumps into that position, you should move in and encourage him to *confess his sins*. You tell him that it'll be all right, and it's good that he has acknowledged what he's done.

It was clear that she loved him. I reassured her, again, that he loved her, too, and was sorry for what was happening. Her confession came despite knowing the consequences.

She was ultimately sentenced to two years in prison. She gave birth to that 14-year-old boy's father's baby before starting her time. The whole case was (to put it mildly) unfortunate. I wish I could have criminally charged the father for contributing to the delinquency of a minor and

Confession Mode

blackmail because, in my opinion, he did more damage to his son than Reynolds. But Reynolds was done with me; she wasn't going to testify against the father; he was her baby's daddy. The 14-year-old boy's family had already been torn apart, and he (the son) was a focal point. Despite the fact his father had done what he had done, he still loved him. I wasn't going to make him testify against him; he didn't want to testify against him. The father walked away without a blemish. He didn't care (in my opinion) about what he had done.

Despite all that, if I had gone in as a son-of-a-bitch and treated Reynolds as some criminal sex offender, she may have never confessed. If I'd gone in with that attitude of *oh, yeah, baby you had yourself some young male ass* when she actually loved and cared for him, if I'd been dismissive about the emotional aspects of this case, who knows how the interrogation would have gone? I suspect she would have told me to screw myself and that would've been the end of it.

More often than not, the sex offender actually *loves* his victim and his definition of *love* is valid (to him).

> ***Oxford Dictionary of Current English (Third Edition 2001) definition of love: 1 a strong feeling of affection; 2 a strong feeling of affection linked with sexual attraction; 3 a great interest and pleasure in something.***

Questions/Discussion Points

Try to understand the other perspective. Articulate and defend a thief's justification for stealing.

Chapter 31
I'm a wild animal in a civilized world

Whenever you observe body language that's inconsistent with the words being spoken, you need to make a mental note of it. If someone denies something while simultaneously crossing his arms and leaning away from you, he's creating a barrier; he's protecting himself because his sympathetic system has been activated. The accusatory question is a threat to the guilty person. That accusatory question is that bear in the woods; should he run or fight? His verbal denials are inconsistent with his physical reaction.

If innocent, he shouldn't feel threatened by the accusatory question and create barriers. Then again, he could be freaked out by being accused of something that he had absolutely nothing to do with and can't understand why he's being accused and is retreating.

> **Nothing in the science of deception is absolute. Nothing.**

I recently observed a suspect nod *yes* when he was verbally denying the allegation that he had taken something. His nod was inconsistent with his words; he should have been shaking his head side to side. At the end of the investigation, he was indeed found innocent of the allegations against him, but that nod was a fascinating anomaly. It certainly piqued my interest at the time I observed it. However, it was just one indicator of deception. He had many other indicators indicating that he was being truthful. The many outweighed the one.

90

> *Never become overly focused on one deceptive behavior at the cost of ignoring all the positive indicators of truthfulness.*

I should clarify an important aspect of the autonomic nervous system: deception and anger are very similar in their physical manifestations. If you accuse an innocent father of raping his daughter, he may very well recoil into a defensive position. It's not that he's guilty and trying to unconsciously protect himself, he's just trying not to punch you in the face.

Fight, flight, or freeze.

Questions/Discussion Points

Entertain this: we have a tendency to know what we know because we "know it." Explain how you know the world is round.

Chapter 32
I'm hearing voices

When I instruct people during the Crisis Intervention Team training, I often encourage them to listen to their interviews and/or interrogations. If I have people who don't conduct interviews (there are non-law enforcement people in the class; first responders), I encourage them to record themselves. I want them to know how they sound to other people. If you've never done it, when you hear yourself for the first time, it's an eye opener. Your voice sounds different to yourself than to others because, when you hear yourself speaking, a large portion of what you're hearing (your voice and it's tone and pitch) is through the bone conduction of your inner ear (the ossicles), which affects the perception of your voice compared to those who are hearing you through the open air and bone conduction.

Furthermore, what's your pacing? Are you a fast talker or a slow talker? What's your pitch? Do you enunciate or are your words slurred together? Do you stumble a lot or say *umm* a lot? You'll be surprised by what you can pick apart.

Recently, I had a defense attorney tell me that I fade off in my volume when I use multisyllable words. He and I have a sort of love/hate relationship. Is he playing with my head or is he being genuine? Back to the audiotape I go.

I've done a lot of television interviews, and they're always nerve wracking for me to watch. But my interviews have improved because I've analyzed every one over the years. I've also learned by studying news broadcasters who have a large national audience. There's a reason they are successful: they've mastered language (tone of voice, pacing) and body presentation. Those people who are successful in the broadcast news industry *appear* trustworthy to their audience.

Usually the successful ones (especially the women) are, by societal standards, attractive. Men are more likely to listen to and accept what a sexy woman (a woman they are attracted to) has to say than an ugly woman. It's no different for women. If a man is sexy, he's okay; a woman will give a handsome man more attention and time. Our bullshit detectors suddenly become fallible when confronted by someone we're attracted to. We'll overlook things (lies, exaggerations and/or embellishments) because we have sex on the brain—*the medulla oblongata (Can I have sex with it? I'd like to have sex with it.).*

It doesn't mean they are trustworthy; it's just about their appearance, how we perceive and hear them. Like it or not, ugly people don't have a long career in the news media.

How many ugly politicians have a long and successful career, if one starts at all?

What's deemed sexually attractive (worthy of reproducing with) is culturally based. Science has proven that there are certain proportions/characteristics to a face/a body that are more desirable than other proportions and/or characteristics.

The aforementioned diatribe was **not** offered to offend, or because I'm a superficial person, a male pig. It was offered because we have primal instincts; we (the interrogators) can't forget that we're still animals. Your suspect is reacting to you on an instinctual level beyond his conscious control.

Questions/Discussion Points

Record yourself having a conversation with people and reading a couple of paragraphs out of a book. Then listen to yourself. What do you hear?

Chapter 33
Flaws, perfections, the political arena, and the psychopath

Watching political debates are a wonderful learning ground for detecting deception. A politician may avoid a question by going onto a different topic. If that politician is good, you'll hardly notice. He'll do it with a smile because he's engaging and entertaining; he'll often use humor. A question may be repeated to stall for time when he's trying to create an answer.

A suspect, during an interrogation, and a politician, during a debate, have one thing in common: someone is paying attention to their every word. Politicians are often required to answer complex questions quickly and in a short period of time. They are under stress, which has activated their autonomic nervous system: they can't flee; they better not freeze because that will look horrendous to the viewers of the debate; so, they'll answer their questions as quickly as possible (to appear in control/knowledgeable/confident), which can create those inadvertent embellishments, white lies, or exaggerations. The politician is experiencing the same stress as a suspect being interrogated.

Many successful politicians and businessmen have anti-social personality traits; they don't necessarily meet the criteria for a diagnosis of anti-social personality, but they may have some of the traits. The anti-social personality knows what the laws are but disregards them; he doesn't care how his decisions will affect other people; he wants what he wants when he wants it (id). That's a very simplistic definition, but it suffices. The anti-social personality has more traits that give him that official diagnosis.

However, politicians and businessmen often have to make decisions that adversely affect others. In order to make those decisions, they have to possess a certain level of emotional disconnect, like an anti-social personality, like a law enforcement officer. We all have elements of some psychiatric diagnosis. I'm prone to mania, but I'm not manic, not clinically.

Often anti-social personalities are mixed in with psychopaths; however, there's a distinct difference, in my opinion, between a psychopath and an anti-social personality (which a lot of criminals in prison are). The psychopath is the anti-social personality on steroids. In my opinion, a psychopath is a subset of the anti-social personality disorder. In simple terms, a violent anti-social personality is a psychopath. The psychopath has absolutely no regard for human life: end of subject. He'd just as soon hurt you as engage you in a conversation.

A psychopath isn't necessarily an obvious monster. He can blend into society. People may be attracted to him. A successful serial killer isn't necessarily a socially outward freak, or he would have likely been apprehended long before he became that infamous serial killer.

Ted Bundy, for example, was a law student who worked for a governor's re-election campaign in Florida, and, at one time, he worked for a Suicide Hotline Crisis Center in Washington State. He was a handsome, intelligent, and soft-spoken man. He was very persuasive; his voice was calm and reassuring.

James Dobson (an evangelical priest and psychologist) interviewed Bundy on January 24, 1989, 24 hours prior to Bundy's execution. Bundy attributed his self-admitted 30 murders to pornography. Every now and then, I could observe Bundy smiling during specific inquiries. But, and this is merely my opinion,

Dobson wanted to attribute Bundy's murders to something like pornography and alcohol instead of acknowledging that Bundy was spiritually evil. So Bundy told Dobson what he thought Dobson wanted to hear.

There's a psychopath, at least I believe him to be one, who I've interviewed a couple times over the years. There's little doubt, in my professional opinion, that he's responsible for the deaths of at least two people. He's engaging. He's polite, but, when I become accusatory, he has no problem looking at me and saying,

"I'm done talking with you. You can leave now."

Once, he even stated that I was probably recording him in hopes of getting him to say something incriminating. He's no fool. He's very calculating and charismatic.

Fortunately, most of the criminals we're tasked with inter-rogating aren't psychopaths. I sincerely doubt that you can get a confession from a true psychopath using my techniques, unless he wanted to confess for his own amusement.

Nonetheless, the successful interrogator should have the ability to think like a criminal, an anti-social personality. At the very least, the interrogator has to accept that criminals do what they do because they want to. They do what they do because they are mo-tivated without regard for the consequences, but in their minds, their motivations were valid.

Regardless, they may be willing to negotiate the terms of their confession; they are looking out for themselves and no one else.

Freud's id: **Want.**

Maslow's esteem: Wanting friendship/**understanding.**

Questions/Discussion Points

It won't be popular but discuss beauty and how it affects personal interactions.

Chapter 34
I won't invite you to my house, but I'll have coffee with you

Before you start an interview/interrogation, you'll need to acknowledge your biases, your preconceived notions of the suspect (you've seen his criminal history), and any possible disdain for him which you may have.

Trust me, if you go into an interrogation loathing the suspect, the likelihood of obtaining a confession will be hovering around zero.

If you go in visibly angry, forget about it.

The interrogator's job is not about telling the suspect what a piece of crap he is; it's about obtaining the truth.

Questions/Discussion Points

Discuss ego; we all have one. What's yours?

Discuss how a thief could be a very effective loss/prevention officer. Discuss how a preferential pedophile* may be an exceptional caregiver.

---

* A preferential pedophile is one who has a specific liking for a particular age range, hair color, or sex. A situational pedophile prefers to have sex with an adult partner but when aroused will seek sexual relief with whomever is available.

Chapter 35
Don't elicit guilt ...

It works the other way as well: you can't allow a suspect's well-connected standing in the community to affect you. He may be wealthy, highly educated, and a philanthropist but don't allow those factors sway you into believing that he must be innocent. Just because he's a successful politician or businessman doesn't mean he's not capable of criminal behavior. A person is a person; no one is without flaw.

Bad is what it is. Good is what it is. It's a matter of perspective, good or bad. It's what it is, human behavior.

If I want information from a Crip gang member, I'll treat him with respect to get what I want. I'll undoubtedly increase my air of authority because violent criminals look at people somewhat simply: can I take him? So, I'm more likely to wear my hostage negotiation uniform, which is S.W.A.T. in its appearance, rather than a tie and slacks. Nonetheless, what's the final goal? I want to obtain enough information that will put him into prison if he's indeed guilty of whatever I'm investigating.

To obtain a confession, I'll want to *change* the suspect's perception of who I am and what I'm trying to elicit. I'm **not** trying to elicit **guilt**, so I can put him into prison; I'm just trying to elicit the **truth**: why he did what he did because it's only fair that I understand his *valid motive*, and I'll do it with respect.

The suspect should have your undivided attention. It's important that you use your active listening skills. If you're distracted, the suspect will notice. If he perceives that you aren't focused on him, he'll likely shut down.

It should be obvious, but I don't want to ignore the obvious. If you have a cell phone on your person, turn it off. I've witnessed too many interrogations go south because of a cell phone ringing and, worse yet, the interrogator answering it. That includes reading and responding to text messages. The suspect must be the sole focus of your attention. Furthermore, you have to be willing to hear, without passing judgment, what the suspect has to say. Toward that end, you must know and accept your limitations prior to starting the interview.

In November 2009, I investigated a drive-by shooting that involved two gang members. I reached out to our gang task force. When it came time to interrogate one of the suspects, who was under arrest for the shooting, I had Investigator Candace Jones and Investigator Chris Hartless available because they had much more knowledge about the gang culture than I did; they worked in the Staunton Augusta Waynesboro Gang Task Force. It was their knowledge of the Crips that allowed for a far more effective inter-rogation. I knew when to exit the interrogation room and let them take the lead. It was that cooperation between departments/ disciplines that led to two gang members receiving 16-year prison sentences.

One of the gang members was clearly a psychopath (my opinion); he accepted his consequences without any emotion; he never violated his *code of silence*. He simply told me *to do what I had to do*. The other gang member was more of an anti-social personality. He demonstrated *emotion* about being caught. He never demonstrated remorse for his actions, which nearly killed an elderly woman; he was focused on himself and his consequences, (prison); he quickly snitched on his accomplice.

> *Never let your ego get in the way. There are times when someone is more suited for the interrogation than you.*

Questions/Discussion Points

Discuss the concept: elicit truth not guilt.

Chapter 36
Yeah, she'll be talking about the sexy stuff

Obviously, at some point, you'll introduce the primary reason why you want to speak to the suspect. I recommend softening the accusation. You don't have to say that you're investigating the **rape** of little Jane.

I often introduce the topic with:
You know little Jane, right?
(Suspect: Yes) *She's a cute kid.* (Suspect: Yes)
Then, I'll say:
She's made statements of a sexual nature, specifically about you. I don't know what to make of them yet, but they are compelling. She disclosed during a forensic interview that involved me, the Commonwealth's Attorney, and a trained psychologist observing from another room. She was very compelling in her subtle details. So, yes, I'm investigating a sexual issue. I've investigated hundreds. (I'm letting him know that I'm an expert in these matters.) *Obviously, since I'm involved, there's a criminal component. I know that this is awkward, but I do appreciate you taking the time to talk with me.*

The proverbial cat is out of the bag. But, I haven't given him any details. I haven't provided him with what I know. I've remained non-accusatory.

Furthermore, when interrogating someone about a sex offense against a child, I always introduce the fact that the child victim will be going into counseling, months of counseling. And, don't we all know how children will embellish their stories? It's only natural. Don't we all know some high school quarterback who's made his mediocre success in high school into some Super Bowl narrative?

The therapist is a mandated reporter and will have to share any and all new information with me. By saying that to the suspect, I've planted a large seed of concern: what else will the victim disclose? A child victim rarely discloses everything in the beginning. That child doesn't fully understand what has happened to him. Disclosure is a lengthy process. Sometimes, when that child is on the witness stand, we'll learn details of the crime not previously known.

I can use the same tactic with a larceny suspect by sharing with him that, in several weeks, all the results from the forensic lab will be made available to me. What may those results show?

I know that I've been using a sexual battery case for an example; however, the same rules apply for any type of case: grand larceny, malicious wounding, murder, or shoplifting. You first build a rapport, and when it comes time to confront the suspect with the crime, you should minimize the crime. In the case of murder, you can say that you are investigating the death of John Smith; you don't have to say that you're investigating the brutal and senseless murder of John Smith. In the case of shoplifting, you can say that you're looking into removal of some items from a store. You don't have to say that he stole some expensive jewelry from a store.

You want to minimize because everyone wants to save face.

For a successful larceny confession, you don't necessarily need the suspect to say that he *stole* the jewelry from a store. If he's admitted to being in the store at the time of the larceny and he's admitted to possessing the jewelry that was reported stolen, does it really matter if he used the word *stolen*? His admissions satisfy the elements of larceny. It'll be up to the defense to argue intent. Oh sure, *maybe he just forgot to pay for it.* It's nice to have the suspect confess to his intent, but sometimes you'll just have to present to the magistrate or commonwealth attorney what you have without the suspect's expressed intent. The physical facts of the case and his admissions will usually suffice for a successful prosecution.

There's an old but true statement: there are two sides to every story. I often tell suspects that when I have five witnesses, I'll have five stories. Sure, the core element of what was seen is fairly consistent, but there are always little details that may vary from witness to witness. It's important for **me** to understand those little inconsistencies, because I understand that no one is perfect. I've even known victims to exaggerate things; I'll tell the suspect that something obviously occurred, which probably shouldn't have happened, and I think the victim may have blown some things out of proportion. I want to hear his version.

Questions/Discussion Points

Discuss why five witnesses will have five different versions of the same event. Can stereotypes and prejudices influence a person's perception of what he witnessed?

Chapter 37
You might be a little bit screwed

How you approach the criminal allegation is a huge hurdle. You could have done everything else correctly and blow it with the introduction of the criminal complaint. So, I suggest that you minimize it. I'm not suggesting that you lie or deceive. Frankly, in this area, you want to be honest or you might find a defense attorney coming after you in court. You can let the suspect know that *there are criminal matters that need to be addressed. Certainly, there are consequences.*

I don't have to necessarily tell the suspect that a conviction *will* result in a 20-year prison sentence. If he asks for more information, I'm justified in stating that it all depends on his criminal history, whether or not he's convicted of these or lesser allegations. Maybe he'll be found innocent. There are so many guidelines and possibilities. That's all true, and I'll continually remind the suspect that I haven't come to any conclusions; all I can do is present everything to the Commonwealth's Attorney.

It's no different than strategies used in hostage negotiations: **you never promise the person, with who you're negotiating, anything that you can't deliver.** Regardless, the decision to provide or deny anything depends on someone else, a superior. You're just the middle man, trying to do what you can, just like a salesman.

You want to be casual, but firm and confident, through this process. The suspect is watching you as much as you're watching him. You're not the only one looking for deception.

I remember a case when the accused, who had an extensive criminal history, asked me if he would be able to get bond that night. I knew that he wouldn't. As much as I wanted to lie and say that he might get bond (the *I just don't know* approach), because I thought that *little lie* might help elicit a confession, I was upfront with him and told him that he'd most likely being going to jail; *I just didn't see a Magistrate giving him a bond.* He stated that he appreciated my honesty because he **knew** that he was going to jail. He'd been through the system many times; he'd been to prison more than once. He stated that if I'd told him otherwise, he would have known that I was *jerking* him around. He asked if I would allow him a smoke before going in front of the magistrate. He smoked; he confessed.

Questions/Discussion Points

Why is it seemingly easier to lie to a child than an adult?

Why might it be harder to lie to a convicted felon than to a non-criminally involved person?

Chapter 38
Will you kindly shut up?

After the suspect has given me his account of events or his alibis, it's time for me to take control. From the moment I become accusatory, I want to stop his denials. If I see him (his mouth beginning to form the word *no*) or hear him coming out with a denial, I stop him. I interrupt with: *I've been respectful; I've listened to you: but, I must respectfully stop you because I want you to listen to me now.*

The suspect may offer some objection, but I firmly persist with *stop, listen.* If he is, indeed, innocent, he'll leave much sooner than later. The longer a suspect stays with you during this process, the more likely that he's guilty.

One of the easiest ways to indicate your desire for the suspect to stop speaking is to just hold up your hand, **stop**. Don't point with a finger. People find that gesture offensive and aggressive. You want to hold up your hand, palm facing the suspect, with all four fingers together. You want to stop him before he utters further words of denials. Interrupt him. The more often he can utter his words of denial, the more difficult it will become to get him to proffer the truth.

You're in control and the suspect needs to know that inconsistencies and denials will no longer be accepted. Don't holler or scream. Remember: someday your interrogation may be played for a judge or jury. If you're yelling and screaming, you'll be giving the defense a legitimate argument for you having coerced a confession out of his client. Juries have seen those Hollywood movies. Don't give them anything to grasp onto as far as you being a son-of-a-bitch, bad cop.

Proper Hand Stop   **Improper Hand Stop**

Questions/Discussion Points

Discuss how law enforcement may interpret an interrogation vs those who may sit on a jury.

Chapter 39
I didn't do this, but I did that

I have absolutely no problem testifying on the stand about what the defendant did or did not say during an interrogation. The Commonwealth's Attorney will obviously ask me, *Did you have an opportunity to speak with John Smith?* I'll say, *Yes*, and he'll follow up with, *Did he say anything to you?* And I will tell the Jury, while looking at them, that the defendant admitted to one thing but denied another thing.

> *Always look at the jury when testifying; it helps build a personal connection between you and the jury that increases your perceived credibility.*

To make it more concrete: I will say that John Smith, the grandfather, admitted to putting his hands down his granddaughter's underwear and touching her vaginal area; however, he denied penetrating her vagina with his fingers.

Once I had an Assistant Commonwealth's Attorney tell me, after a conviction in a case, that I shouldn't have told the jury what the grandfather denied. My rebuttal was: The defense is going to follow-up with that question anyway. The defense has heard the confession: so, let me be up front and honest with the jury. I would like to take the wind out of the defense's sails by stating, as the investigator in this case, the grandfather denied (to me) penetration, but rest assured, he admitted to putting his hands down his granddaughter's underwear and touching her vaginal area.

The granddaughter has already testified that her grandfather put his hands down her underwear and penetrated her *monkey*. I've testified that the grandfather admitted to doing something that a grandfather should never do. Usually, the defense will have minimal follow-up questions, because I've already honestly testified to what his client had admitted to and denied. Granddad's admission lends credibility to the victim and my acknowledgment of his denials lends credibility to me. My final argument to that Assistant Commonwealth's Attorney was: If I withheld his denials (as pathetic as they were), would I not appear deceptive to the Jury?

It's about my credibility in court. It's about my reputation.

It's about truth.

Questions/Discussion Points

What is your role as witness on the stand? Is it to paint a complete picture or to connect just a few dots?

Chapter 40
It's O.K. to horse around with horses

The Jerry Sandusky case (the former assistant, Penn State football coach now convicted of molesting children) is in the media forefront as I write this. He was interviewed by Bob Costas on November 15, 2011 and asked: *Are you sexually attracted to children?*

It took him over 15 seconds to answer that question. He also responded to the question by repeating the question, which is a delay tactic. It's not necessarily a conscious one, but his brain was trying to juggle many things.

An innocent person has to focus on one thing when asked a question: the past. Did he do it or not? So, the innocent person has a quick scan of his memory, and there's no memory of what he's being accused (past). So, he answers with a timely, *no*. The guilty person has a lot to juggle: He's currently being accused of a crime that could result in imprisonment (future); he has to wander through his memory that holds an account of what he's being accused of (past), and he must successfully deny that which he knows is true (present). Then, and only then, he must say, *no*. Again, it took Sandusky a lot of time to answer a question that most of us would have had no problem answering with a quick and resounding, *No*.

In that Costas interview, Sandusky further stated, "*I have horsed around with kids. I have showered after workouts. I have hugged them, and I have touched their legs without intent of sexual contact.*"

115

He also admits, later in the interview, that, "*He shouldn't have showered with those kids.*"

He admits, "*We* (He's referring to a 10-year-old boy and himself) *were showering and horsing around ...*"

He admits to having *horsed around* with a child, while naked, in a shower.

I won't belabor the point, but what's an adult male doing showering with children who are not part of his immediate family? Now, I'll take it a step further: how many adult males shower with their 10-year-old child and horse around? A good follow-up question for Sandusky would have been: What do you mean by *horsing around*?

Questions/Discussion Points

Discuss the pitfalls of accepting the suspect's terminology based on your own experiences and education.

What does "horsing around" mean to you?

What did it mean to Sandusky?

Chapter 41
If you ask someone if he committed a crime, and he hems and haws before answering, that's a clue

You and the suspect are speaking. You've addressed the victim's allegations against the suspect. You've been paying attention to his body language, his eyes, his carotid and radial arteries, and how he answers your questions. Finally, you ask him the relevant question, the accusatory question: Does he actually answer your question?

If you ask the suspect if he did the crime and he replies: *I'm a good person; I'm a Christian, I would never do something like that.* That's not an answer; he has **not** answered your question. He didn't say *no*.

Furthermore, when a person denies something, it's important that you know what he's denying. Don't assume you know a person's vocabulary.

I briefly had a case in which a six-year-old girl had disclosed to a school counselor that her daddy had sex with her. The counselor did the right thing by notifying Child Protective Services who, in turn, notified me. Immediately, a forensic interview was scheduled. The distraught mother brought her daughter to the Valley Children's Center. During the forensic interview, it was quickly learned that the girl's definition of sex was: daddy had kissed her on the lips. No crime had been committed.

So, when a man tells me he was merely tickling his daughter, I'll ask him for clarification. What does he mean by *tickling?* I'll have him describe tickling to me. Tickling means different things to different people. Tickling can be innocent; or, tickling can be a grooming process. Does the suspect's act of tickling fit *innocently* (within your professional and/or personal life experience) within the scenario provided by him and the victim?

The core of hostage and crisis negotiation is about allowing the suspect to *save face*. When we make a mistake, we'll try to portray ourselves in the best light. What's the easiest out? Remember Maslow's *esteem* stage of development? We seek friendship. We want people to like us.

Therefore, offer him possibilities: He committed the crime because it was necessary to provide for something (Maslow; a need; to feed his family), or it was an act of uncontrollable impulses (id; a moment presented itself; alcohol or drugs); or the suspect just didn't give a damn about the consequences (ego). Most people don't buy into that last one; no one really wants to admit to blatantly not giving a damn; so, the suspect is more likely to entertain the two previous possibilities. He either committed the crime because he didn't care, **or** he did what he did because of a desire or need (a bad impulse).

> *It's about options. One option is more acceptable than the other; but, regardless of the one chosen, a confession has been obtained. We like options because they give us a sense of control, and we like control. Give the suspect what he wants (a chance to save face), and you'll increase your odds of obtaining the truth. Let the suspect have the opportunity to blame his more primitive instincts for the crime committed. Give him the opportunity to acknowledge that he understands higher reasoning (ego or super ego).*

I can honestly say to a pedophile or a rapist that I have something in common with him: *I understand what it's like to desire something I know I shouldn't have.* There's a $600 guitar I want right now. I really can't afford it. I could purchase it with a credit card. I shouldn't (ego), but the temptation is there; it exists. I could succumb to that temptation (id).

I'll also make the victim into something he wasn't. I've portrayed a six-year-old child as a sexual curious creature because children are inquisitive.

I've made a rape victim into a troubled woman who kind of got what she got.

With a petit larceny case, I'll have no problem telling a suspect that the victim was a *dumb ass* for leaving his wallet in an unlocked car; *he was just asking for it.* It wasn't like the suspect was looking to commit a crime; *the opportunity just presented itself.*

You just can't overplay the victim's culpability; you have to be subtle, realistic. I described that 6-year-old as sexually *curious*, not sexually active. I didn't call the woman a slut; I called her *troubled*.

Raping a *troubled* person is no different than raping an upstanding member of the community. Force is force; rape is rape. However, a suspect is more likely to confess to raping a person, if that person is presented as having some responsibility for what happened. I've warned the victim of rape and her family about what they may hear during my interrogation, when it's played for the judge or jury.

Rest assured, once the suspect acknowledges force (an element of the rape), we'll discuss how, despite whatever perceived culpability the victim may or may not have had, his actions were inappropriate/criminal.

The id got the better of his ego.

Questions/Discussion Points

Discuss how victims of crime may have increased the likelihood of their victimization because of their behavior, i.e., people who leave their vehicles unlocked.

Chapter 42
Sometimes a spade is a spade

There'll be a time in the interrogation when the suspect has clearly lied to me. I'll know he's lied based on the facts, based on my knowledge of the case, and it'll be time to call a spade a spade—and confront that lie. I can help the suspect save face by not blatantly calling him a *liar*.

Liar is an aggressive word; most people instinctively recoil at being called a liar; that accusation triggers the autonomic nervous system, the medulla oblongata, that reptilian brain. Calling someone a liar is a threat to him. The suspect's sympathetic system will kick in with that fight or flight response.

I'll approach inconsistencies (a nice way of calling a lie a lie without using that loaded word, *liar*) by letting the suspect know that **I'm** having trouble making sense of what he's telling me; I want to understand; so, he needs to help me. It's **not his fault** that I'm not connecting the dots. I'll make my point clear (he knows that I'm declaring bullshit) without activating/alerting his instinctual need to fight or flee; I'm asking for his assistance. I'll even apologize for not understanding.

Don't throw all his inconsistencies at him at once. Pick one and ask him about it. You don't want to overwhelm him with everything that's indicating that he's a liar. Ease him into accepting (for himself) that his fabricated story (lie) has fallen apart. Start with the lesser element of the crime. For example, in a rape case, you can start by addressing his kissing of the woman. Men and women kiss. It sounds romantic, harmless enough. Of course when you kiss, you become aroused and will touch her breasts. *I can certainly understand that. That makes sense.*

If you have a fact, a piece of evidence, that discredits the suspect's story, you should introduce it gently. Again, you don't want to unnecessarily activate that reptilian brain. Just introduce the evidence without any fanfare. I'm against the big show of throwing evidence into his face. Let the suspect know that you have this factual piece of the puzzle and maybe he can help you understand why what he's presented is inconsistent with the known fact.

Could he have made a mistake? We all make mistakes. Memory is fallible.

I'll use an aggravated battery for an example: A victim, Arnold, has been beaten senseless with a blunt item; he received 16 stitches but is otherwise alright; he's identified Derek Kellog as the assailant; Kellog has been friends with the victim for years; they are drinking buddies. The suspect has initially denied causing the victim's injuries; he's stated Arnold was drunk and fell and hit his head on a railing. I'm at the point where Kellog has acknowledged some inconsistencies and is revising his story. So, at this time, I may introduce my *feeling* that Arnold was not as much of a victim as he's portrayed himself to me.

Hell, 16 stitches ain't the biggest deal in the world. My kid got 4 stitches a couple months ago while skateboarding with a friend who accidentally knocked him down (a lie). Damn, Arnold is really making you into some kind of bad guy, and, from what I've seen, you're pretty decent. But, I can see how things may have gotten out of control.

The truth always lies in the middle, somewhere. *Maybe, you all had too much to drink, and Arnold said something that angered you, upset you? Maybe, he pushed you first.* I'm offering options that put some responsibility on the victim and take some off the suspect, Kellog.

> *Lies always have a foundation in elements of truth.*

Again, it's about saving face. I've introduced a story about my child who received stitches (a lie); most adults can relate to some kind of story involving silly childhood injuries (a truth). I've placed some responsibility for what happened on the victim by stating that the victim was trying to make Kellog into a bad guy when it was just a drunken misunderstanding. I've given Kellog something to work with, something that will allow him to present himself in the best possible light while still eliciting a confession.

We like to be genuinely understood.

Questions/Discussion Points

Discuss a mistake you have made, something shameful. You have to be comfortable in your own fallible skin to be an effective interrogator.

Chapter 43
Dog talk—I talk

So much of what I've written about during these previous pages can be related to training an animal. You'll have a lot more success training your dog with positive reinforcement than with punishment. B. F. Skinner (a behaviorist) did a lot of research in the area of positive reinforcement with rats (operant conditioning). Every time your dog does something you want it to do, you should give it a treat (like Skinner did with his rats/positive reinforcement) or affection. If all you do is beat your dog (punish it/punishment) when it does something wrong, you'll really get nowhere. Sure, the dog will learn what not to do, but it won't learn what to do and become neurotic and a real pain in the ass. When a suspect finally admits to some portion of the crime, you should reinforce him with positive words like: *thank you; now, I can start making sense of things.*

I joke about ***dog talk interrogations*** with my family; we have a muttly mutt dog, and my son laughs when I talk to it with a soothing voice (a playful voice) while calling her the *ugliest, most worthless creature on the planet.* I'm rubbing and petting her. I'm smiling. I'm calling her *slug bait.* Everything about me is open and reinforcing; however, my words are mean. Serena, our dog, doesn't know that. Everything that I'm doing is making her happy. Her tail is wagging. She's on her back so I can rub her belly; all the while, I'm teasingly calling her a variety of vile things.

People are not that much different than dogs (or Skinner's rats). Earlier, I mention that the vast majority of communication between people doesn't involve the actual meaning of words; it's our body language; it's our tone of voice; it's our facial expressions.

If you keep that in mind, you can call a liar a **liar** without (necessarily) offending him.

It's all in how you approach it, how you say it (word it), the accusation. You should use the most positive wording possible to illustrate/articulate your doubt about a suspect's denials. You don't have to be sickly sweet. I'm not talking about being all buddy/ buddy with him. But, you don't have to be in his face. All you have to do is be **nonjudgmental** in expressing your doubt. If you're expressing your doubt in a manner that allows for positive reinforcement, you're more likely to obtain a truthful statement from him, the suspect who you believe is lying.

As a general rule of thumb (referring to operant conditioning/ behavior modification), you should give a person at least three statements of positive reinforcement for every negative statement (every statement of doubt) given. Stroke the suspect. Think of him as a rat. Like it or not, we are animals. We respond easily to positive reinforcement, and we fear punishment.

Punishment* doesn't make the suspect do what you want him to do: tell the truth. It just makes him fearful and defensive: activating his autonomic nervous system. If he's defensive, he's more likely to continue lying.

During the interview process, when you're establishing a rapport, it's important to note if there are any topics or words that cause the suspect discomfort; it's worth noting them because they may be important if you find yourself interrogating him later.

Certainly, there are words you want to avoid all together (whenever possible) because some words immediately cause alarm. *Liar* is obviously one of them. *Murder, rape, criminal, prison, sex*

---

* A penalty imposed for wrongdoing. Rough handling; mistreatment (*The American Heritage Dictionary of the English Language*, 4th edition, ©2000, by Houghton Mifflin Company.

offender, pedophile, pervert, low life, and *thief* are others; that's a short list, but I want you to think about the words to avoid when interviewing or interrogating a person.

Questions/Discussion Points

Discuss words or descriptors that could offend a suspect. Which words or descriptors offend you?

Chapter 44
Epithelial cells and that damn scar on your palm

The Supreme Court has continually supported law enforcement's right to lie or deceive a suspect during an interrogation (*Frazier v. Cupp,* 394 U.S. 731, 739 1969). You can't lie about Miranda; you can't lie about the letter of the law; you can't make promises about the outcome of the case if the suspect was to confess. But you can lie and deceive about evidence that you may or may not have. However, you want to be careful. If the suspect catches you in a lie or he knows you're lying, you might as well end the interrogation; your credibility and any rapport established will be lost.

If you tell a suspect that you found his prints at the crime scene, but he knows that he wore latex gloves, the game is over.

If you tell a suspect that you have him inside the store on the surveillance tape but he was actually outside (driving the getaway car), the game is over. Maybe the suspect knows there wasn't any surveillance because he'd already done his research; so never bluff about video surveillance evidence if there wasn't a surveillance system set up.

If you tell a suspect that you found his sperm inside the five-year-old-girl, but all he did was digitally penetrate her ...

It's better to approach the issues of evidence with: *I've retrieved videotape from the store and sent it off to the lab for digital enhancement and analysis. Is there any reason I might see you in that video surveillance?* I didn't tell the suspect what areas of the store were under surveillance. I haven't committed myself to anything.

I'll approach fingerprints in the same manner by telling the suspect that I've recovered numerous prints, and some partial prints, and had them sent off to the lab for analysis. *Is there any reason his prints will be discovered?* Again, I haven't committed to anything. That, and if the suspect was wearing latex gloves, I may have triggered a little concern by introducing *partial prints*. Could his glove have torn, if he was wearing a glove?

Is it possible any of your DNA will be discovered on that girl's body?

The more comfortable I've become with the art of interrogating people the less I lie to them, especially regarding evidence. However, in May 2009, I assisted the Nelson County Sheriff's Office, an adjoining county, with a murder. An elderly lady had been brutally stabbed over 20 times, in her home; her car was later located in the city of Waynesboro, approximately 30 minutes away. Two people of interest were established because of a Crime Stoppers report. All that had been reported was that someone had thought that he had seen two people (*who kind of/sort of looked like these two guys*) in the area of the victim's residence around the time she may have been stabbed. The Nelson County Sheriff's Office, based on that information, determined four things of importance: Where the victim's car was located was in the proximately of one of the suspect's mother's residence; the victim had known one of the suspects (she'd been a beloved teacher in the community); one of the suspects lived within a mile of the victim; and both suspects were known associates.

It wasn't much to go on at all, but it was interesting information. Furthermore, Nelson County was familiar with the two individuals; they had an extensive history of drug- and alcohol-related issues.

Sheriff David Brooks allowed me and Investigator Becky Adcock to interview the suspects.

We located one of the individuals, Langley, and he agreed to come to the Nelson County Sheriff's Office to be interviewed.

Sheriff Brooks bought him a sandwich. Sharing food or drink with someone is an exceedingly strong rapport builder. It costs very little money, but that purchase can go a long way. If you buy me a drink at a bar, I'm more likely to talk with you. At the very least, I'll feel obligated to talk with you.

*It would be rude to **not** speak with the purchaser of my drink.*

Even though Langley wasn't in custody, he was Mirandized; sometimes, you really want to *dot your I's and cross your T's.* This was (after all) a capital murder case. Like it or not, a good defense attorney improves your odds in court. In a capital murder case, there are going to be a lot of attorneys involved.

I already knew that some partial prints had been recovered from the victim's car, and a palm print had also been recovered from the dashboard. It appeared from that palm print that who-ever had left it may have had a cut or scar in the palm of his hand.

I started my interview and noticed that Langley did have a cut in the palm of his hand, but I didn't mention it. Once I'd established his alibi, I asked him if he had ever been in the victim's car, and he responded that he had not. I introduced the palm print with the obvious scar. Would it be possible, once the lab had analyzed the print, that it could be identified as coming from him? At that point, he paused before responding; he then remembered that he'd been in her car two weeks earlier. He'd been in her house, visiting, when she'd asked him to go to her car to retrieve something. That might be how his print had wound up in the car.

Now, the suspect has, at least, put himself in the victim's car.

I then remembered something Detective Ben Lemons (from the Waynesboro Police Department) had told me months before: he'd obtained a confession from a child sex offender by discussing epithelial cells. I went with it. I thanked the suspect for helping me; now, I could understand how his palm print wound up in the car. I asked him if he knew about epithelial cells; he stated that he didn't. I explained that they were skin cells. We lose millions every day. It's kind of like dandruff; your skin is constantly flaking off. He understood and accepted that concept. That much was true: We do lose skin cells all the time. So, I explained to him that we had, of course, recovered all kinds of skin cells from the victim's car (lie). So far, all they had revealed was that they had come from a person of European descent (white) and somewhere in the age of late teens to late twenties (both statements were a lie). My suspect was 19. I proffered that the lab couldn't narrow it down much further, but, certainly, he could understand why I couldn't rule him out, yet; he was white and in the right age range. He accepted that.

I further explained that skin cells degrade over time. The lab can tell how long a skin cell had been at a certain location based on how it degraded. What the lab had discovered was that the cells had been in the victim's car for no more than 48 hours (a lie). So, in summary, I reminded him that his scar appeared to match the palm print found in the car (which would be analyzed later and compared with his), and he'd already admitted to being in the car. I asked: *Is it possible that you are mistaken about when you were in the victim's car?*

I reminded him that he had told us that it was two weeks prior to the victim's death, but the epithelial cell evidence strongly suggested that he had been in the car around the time of the victim's death; I didn't say murder.

I introduced that maybe it was a simple car larceny gone wrong. I blamed the victim for intervening. If she'd just stayed in her bed none of this would be happening right now. I blamed his friend. I made it clear to the suspect that the victim bore some responsibility for her death. His friend bore some responsibility. Whatever happened that early morning was an unfortunate event because she *stupidly* (putting that responsibility on the victim) tried to fight him and fight his friend. *What was she thinking?*

Langley gave up everything but blamed his friend, Wilson, for the actual murder. He was there and witnessed it, but he didn't kill her. He, however, admitted that it had been his idea to go to her residence to steal the victim's car.

Wilson, who was brought in later for questioning, gave up everything too. Like his friend, he admitted only to being there and witnessing it, stating that it was Langley who stabbed the victim. He admitted to cleaning up the murder scene by wiping it down to eliminate any possible prints.

They both admitted that they had spent a couple weeks discussing what it would be like to kill someone.

Regardless, because of their collective statements, all the evidence was recovered: the murder knife that had been thrown into the woods behind one of the suspect's mother's residence; the fire extinguisher that had been used to break into the victim's residence and was thrown alongside a major road in another city;

and the keys to the victim's vehicle, in a street gutter, where they had thrown them after they had ditched the victim's car.

A lot of factors contributed to those successful interrogations and ultimate convictions of Langley and Wilson: the hard work of the Nelson County Sheriff's Office, the Virginia State Police, the Waynesboro Police Department, and the Augusta County Sheriff's Office.

As of August 2011, both Langley and Wilson are serving triple life sentences (each) for her brutal murder.

For what it's worth, toward the end of my interview with the second suspect, Wilson (after I'd obtained his confession), I realized I'd done something that I should've never done: I'd become angry. When I received the transcript to prepare myself for the preliminary hearing, the transcriptionist had actually typed the word **enraged** after my name to indicate my demeanor before speaking.

I should've never lost my composure. I'm minimizing here: the transcriptionist used *enraged*. I'm merely saying that I had only lost my composure.

I'd potentially given the defense something to work with: *He coerced a confession from my client; my client was scared;* the list could go on. Granted, I wasn't *enraged* until the very end, until I'd obtained all the information I needed. I'd even stopped my interrogation shortly after I recognized my anger; however, it could've become an unnecessary distraction had the case gone to trial.

Another important lesson learned from my mistake was: If the last thing a person remembers about you was you yelling at him and being an asshole, the likelihood that he'll speak with you in the future is virtually nonexistent. You've interrogated someone, and he hasn't confessed: you don't have the probable cause to arrest; so, you let him go. Weeks later, you have new information and you've left that suspect on good terms, he may speak with you again. He may (based on the new evidence and the presentation of it) confess. You never know.

You want to keep your options available by maintaining your rapport with that suspect.

Questions/Discussion Points

Discuss the pros and cons of lying to a suspect. What happens if you are caught in a lie?

Chapter 45
If I may be completely honest with you ...

The politically incorrect term for habitual criminals is *frequent fliers*. They are the ones who you're continually arresting. You remember them; they remember you. Not that it's happened often, but I've had people thank me, after their conviction, for being *decent* with them, for *not judging* them. They'd confessed to me, with minimal effort, because I was being respectful.

Your tone of voice and volume are important when interrogating someone. You want to be authoritative but soothing, non-threatening. Your voice can trigger that reptilian brain that is always on alert for a threat.

You want to be calm and calculating in your delivery. If you are about to deceive the suspect with evidence (which you may or may not have), you don't want to be fumbling around. You better be able to convincingly answer any questions he may have about your so-called evidence, such as epithelial cells.

I can't stress it enough, the suspect is listening to and watching you as much as you are listening to and watching him.

Again, I rarely lie about evidence. Sometimes, you may underestimate the suspect's intelligence and/or knowledge of criminal investigations and a lie will permanently destroy any hope of obtaining a confession because he knows you're full of crap.

There are some responses to questions that a suspect may give that will make me want to respond with *bullshit*. Obviously, I don't utter that word or any variation of it (usually), but I will stop the suspect and inform him that his responses don't make sense to me.

Those *I don't recall, not to the best of my knowledge* responses should pique your interest, especially if what you're investigating occurred within the past few days.

Unless a suspect lives in a palatial mansion and entertains hundreds of guests, he should be able to tell you who's been in his house. If a suspect has confirmed that he was at his home on a certain night, and you ask him if a Samantha Fulk was there, and he responds with a *Not to the best of my knowledge*, I'll respond with a firm, *She either was or she wasn't.*

It's no different that the suspect having responded with *I don't think so.* What do you mean, you don't think so? It's a *yes* or *no* question. *She either was* or *she wasn't.* It's an evasive response which requires follow-up questions and/or statements. And to lessen the threat on the suspect, I'll usually continue explaining my incredulity about his vagueness by stating that my experience has taught me that these situations (being questioned by law enforcement) can be nerve-wracking; I understand. I would be nervous, too.

So, Sir (respect), *if I may be so bold, I believe that you do remember Samantha being at your house.* (I'll nod my head up and down; body language; mirroring; I'm encouraging him.) *I've been respectful to you; you've been respectful to me. Clearly, she was there. She's not lying about being there. So tell me what you remember about Samantha being at your house, at your party.*

I've let the suspect know that I **know** that she was at his residence and that he needs to revise his story (tell the truth). I've called him a liar without using that harsh word *liar* and without being hostile. Typically, in order to save face, the suspect will *suddenly* remember Samantha being at his party. He knows that I won't accept anything else but him acknowledging the truth: She was there. It's also important that I don't confront his vague answers with questions. I'll make statements. I'll end my exposure of his lies, his vagueness, with a statement: *Tell me about Samantha being at your house.*

If you end your exposure of the suspect's vagueness with a question, you'll have provided him with the ability to continue being vague. This is an interrogation; you're in control. He needs to be reminded of that.

Once he's officially verbalized that Samantha was in his house, I can start asking questions to clarify what she did while at his house. What did they do together? But, nothing changes. If the suspect gives a vague answer, I'll confront him and end my confrontation with a statement: *You and she talked. Tell me about that conversation.*

Rest assured, an innocent person will not tolerate this and will tell you what you can do with yourself. If Samantha wasn't at his house, your interrogation will end quickly because he'll end it (angrily) with conviction.

If I've said it once, I've stated it numerous times in this book: a guilty person doesn't want to disengage from you until he believes that you believe him. An innocent person will (on average) lawyer up and leave. Use that knowledge to your benefit.

Questions/Discussion Points

Discuss other vague responses; for example, "Not that I can say."

Chapter 46
If only you would leave me alone

This may very well be too much about semantics, but I love *I would have to say "No"* answers.

The suspect hasn't said *no;* the suspect has essentially said that he will have to say *no* because *yes* is (indeed) the right answer but that *yes* (the truth) could get him into trouble. So, to prevent getting into trouble, he'll have to say *no*. *Would* is a conditional verb.

I would have bought a car, if I'd won the lottery.

If I wasn't scared of going to prison, I would tell you that I was at the crime scene.

I would, if I could. I can't, so I won't.

It's really easy to overlook those *I would* statements: ***I would have to say** that I was in New York on New Year's Eve* when asked if he was in Chicago, where the crime occurred. That response isn't stating that he was, indeed, in New York on New Year's Eve. The suspect is merely stating that (given the conditions/the situation) he'll have to say that he was in New York (on New Year's Eve) because that's better than saying where he really was, Chicago. He doesn't want to implicate himself.

With the threat of going to prison, I will have to say I was in New York. If I told you I was in Chicago, you'll figure out that I committed the crime.

Don't let those *I would have to say ...* answers go unchecked. It's semantics; so, it's not definitive. But, you should clarify those responses.

I would, if I could, but I can't.

Chapter 47
It's easier to try, than do

The following answer is really no different than the afore-mentioned answer of *I would have to say* and should also alert you to the possibility of deception:

*I'm **trying** to tell you the truth.*

Trying is vastly different than *doing*. *Doing* doesn't require clarification. You either did or you didn't tell the truth.

People who are innocent **do**; the guilty **try**.

I tried to run a marathon, but I failed.
I ran to the cooler for another beer.

Chapter 48
The innocent are innocent

Another indicator of deception is that *I can honestly say* statement because the guilty will emphasize in order to hide their lies.

Why does the suspect need to clarify his response? Does that declaration of *honestly telling me something* (**now**) mean that he lied about something else earlier? Or, has he been telling me the truth and is now about to lie to me and attempting to disguise that lie with the word *honestly?*

Someone who's telling the truth will be telling the truth; he won't make any attempts at clarifying the truth because (since he's telling the truth) he'll likely assume that you *know* that he's telling the truth.

The guilty person, instead of just saying *No, I didn't do it*, may say variations of: *Absolutely not; I swear on my mother's grave.*

Simply illustrated: If I'm asked if my name is Paul, I'll answer, *Yes*; not, *Absolutely, yes*; not, *If I may be honest, yes.*

Are you the president of the United States? *No*; not, *If I may be honest, no.*

The liar will have that need to clarify his words. He's not assuming, because he's lying, that you're accepting his lies.

Someone who's withholding information (lying) is more likely to say that he's *trying* to tell the truth or that he's being *honest.*

Again, it's your task, as the interrogator, to help that suspect go from *trying to tell the truth* to *telling the truth*.

I'd tell the truth, if I could, but I can't, *honestly.*

The more "blah, blah" that precedes the denial (the no), the more curious I become.

Chapter 49
I didn't take no stinkin' money!

The suspect wants to save face, and you'll have to help him save face for him to tell the truth, to confess. You'll be his priest, his therapist, his parent, whatever it takes to make him comfortable with telling you the truth (that truth that could put him in prison). It's no easy task.

Semantics can be as fun and complicated as you want them; I suggest reading books on the English language. My first real exposure to semantics (as it pertains to questioning someone) was at the Virginia School for Polygraph.

If you're administering a polygraph test on someone regarding the larceny of $1,200, you don't want to ask the examinee if he stole the $1,200.

You'll want to ask the examinee if he *took any of that money*.

First and foremost, *stole* is a strong term. Second, and most important, maybe he didn't take $1,200. Maybe his accomplice took $800 of it, and he took only $400. So he could *truthfully* say that he didn't take $1,200; or (because sometimes it's been known to happen, inadvertently or intentionally) the victim reported the wrong amount of money stolen. Indeed, $1,200 wasn't stolen, it was only $500.

If a suspect is very specific in his denial to the question asked, you should consider a follow-up question. It's like someone responding to the question *Did you drink alcohol last night?* with *I did not drink **one** beer last night.*

The only thing you know for sure is that he didn't drink **one** beer. He may not have drunk any beer or he could have drunk a twelve pack. Maybe he drank a fifth of tequila. It's your responsibility to clarify the suspect's response. Don't assume he denied drinking any alcohol based on that response. Think about it: Let's assume that I drank that fifth of tequila last night (dark tequila and diet soda) and someone asks me if I drank any alcohol last night, I could evasively answer that question with: *Honestly, I didn't drink any beer.*

My friends wouldn't think twice about that answer because I typically drink beer, not tequila.

How much alcohol did you drink?

Chapter 50
You say crap; I say bullshit

In 2003, I responded to a 9-1-1 domestic call. Upon my arrival, I was confronted by a husband and wife. Neither one had any visible injuries, but the wife was tearful and otherwise upset. She was clearly stating that her husband had hit her in the chest. He was adamant that he hadn't. Furthermore, the husband was playing that *I'm your buddy* routine with me.

When a suspect is being overly nice, his friendliness should pique your interest: Why is he being so damn nice? Is he attempting to manipulate you as you would be him: or, is that his basic nature?

The husband ultimately admitted to *shoving* his wife into a wall using the palm of his hand. His attempted demonstration (which wasn't kindly received) clearly represented a striking blow. The wife (and rightfully so) had perceived her husband's actions as being of a *hitting* nature; he'd attempted to portray his actions as merely being a *shove*.

That's the world of semantics and deception. You say *shove;* I say *hit*.

Questions/Discussion Points

The previous four chapter discussed semantics.

Discuss how our education and experiences can create assumptions based on the suspect's vague response. Be sure to clarify the suspect's statements.

Chapter 51
Talk shows, families, and confessions

When you're interviewing and/or interrogating someone, be aware of his language abilities and his understanding of the words you're using. You don't want to talk over his head. It's also important to note if a suspect has any cognitive disabilities: intellectual disability (previously referred to as mental retardation), schizophrenia, anything that could warrant you being exceedingly careful with how you proceed with your interrogation.

> *Someone with an intellectual disability is much more likely to give a false confession because he is very likely to agree with you and act as if he understands everything (your interpretation of events; his culpability) to hide his disability. A schizophrenic's perception of the world is already tainted with hallucinations and can be more easily directed into believing he was involved with something, when he wasn't.*

In 2008, Investigator Jenkins and I had Peter Huffman in custody for impregnating his 14-year-old, biological daughter. He was handcuffed in his residence. He'd been Mirandized. While we waited for the transport vehicle to bring him to the Sheriff's Office, we started our interrogation; we had decided that it was now or never. We wanted to interrogate him before he had a chance to fully realize the gravity of his situation.

Both of us were respectful; we were trying to be understanding. For both of us, that was a challenge; this was, after all, a case of incest. I'd taken the lead role in the interrogation. Huffman was clearly on the verge of confessing, but I was failing to get him to admit to the truth: He was dancing all around the issue, and I was becoming increasingly frustrated. Fortunately, Investigator Jenkins intervened. I hadn't been speaking Huffman's language. I was being *too big worded* in my approach, with my communication. Jenkins approached Huffman more simply; he talked about the *Jerry Springer Show* and that big envelope with those DNA results (*and the baby's daddy is ...*) .

Huffman confessed within minutes. He understood Jerry Springer. He understood and connected with Investigator Jenkins.

Questions/Discussion Points

Discuss how educational differences can create difficulty in establishing rapport.

Chapter 52
Did you hear that?

There's a lot to consider when it comes to the language a suspect uses. But I would be remiss if I didn't explore the scary world of silence. It's damn near universal: People hate silence during a conversation. We want to fill that void (that silence) with words. **Don't.** Let the suspect suffer through his silence. At the most, you can occasionally utter the words *It's ok* to encourage him while he's thinking. Otherwise, stay silent. Let him own the silence, his silence.

It's difficult. Seconds may seem like minutes. If those seconds seem like minutes to you, they'll seem like hours to the suspect, and he'll eventually say something just to end it. The longest period of silence I've ever experienced was approximately three minutes. It was excruciating. I wanted to say something (to ask another question), but I bit my tongue.

When the suspect finally spoke, he started confessing without hesitation (for a reason): he had something to say. The silence was killing him. The silence was applying pressure, not me.

Sometimes silence is more powerful than words spoken.

Chapter 53
Sitcoms and technology

With any interrogation, there are two things that you should keep actively lurking in your mind because you should be recording it: the *first* is the length of the interrogation, and the *second* is the 3 Cs (Calm, Calculated, and in Control).

Most of my successful interrogations have lasted less than one hour.

Remember Barry Johnson, the grandfather who molested his granddaughter and I failed to pick up on his masturbation comment? That interrogation lasted for approximately three hours. For all intents and purposes, I failed with that interrogation. I missed his *possible* masturbation comment which was stated around the 72-minute mark.

Once you've approach that one-hour mark without the interrogation yielding any substantial statements from the suspect, you should consider shutting it down. Either he's innocent or you failed to establish that rapport and things are not likely to improve, and he won't confess. The longer the interrogation lasts, it becomes more likely that you'll provide the defense with an argument for you having badgered his client, coerced a confession from him, or any number of other issues.

False confessions involve a lot of time (much more than an hour) and a hostile environment (sleep deprivation and the lack of food and/or water; physical intimidation; extreme temperature manipulation), and/or false promises. Nonetheless, I'll seriously consider shutting down an interrogation around the one hour mark if the suspect has not proffered any incriminating statements. I'll try to leave on good terms and hope that there'll be another opportunity.

We're a society with short attention spans—cell phones, digital television recorders, lap top computers, iPods, video games, YouTube, Facebook, Twitter, satellite and cable television, and 24-hour news (major military assaults are summarized in minutes). The idea that an interrogation lasted for more than an hour can easily become a problem in court. A half-hour sitcom is quick and easy entertainment, easy to follow without dedicating effort. A two-hour movie is more of a commitment. For a jury, you want the interrogation to fall somewhere in between those two extremes—preferably closer to the sitcom's 30-minute time constraint. Quick and easy.

The longer the jury has to listen to an interrogation, the more likely someone on the jury will tune out and assume the suspect was coerced.

If nothing else, I hope that I've introduced you to the idea of being calm, calculated, and in control. Again (because I've stated it before), you'll make the defense's job difficult if you've elicited a confession from his client while being calm and respectful. You don't want to become *enraged*. You want to have your facts collected (a thorough investigation) and prepared for a calm, but firm, presentation.

You don't want the interrogation to become hostile and heated; you shouldn't be judgmental; you should be calm and cool in your presentation. You want to be calculating with how and when you confront the suspect with his inconsistencies, with the facts.

You're in control.

Questions/Discussion Points

Discuss the three "Cs" (calm, calculated, and in control).

Chapter 54
The Snake Man

In 2009, a seven-year-old girl disclosed that a 70-year-old man, Paul Fredrick, had *kissed* her vagina (*down there*) when he took her out into her parents' field, in a pick-up truck. He had been the family handyman for a couple of years. Everyone spoke highly of him. He'd been accepted into the family. He bought their daughter gifts. He was wonderful with her.

When she disclosed, her parents were devastated by their 20/20 hindsight. Remember McQueary? *20/20 hindsight is brutal.* The father informed me that he remembered reading a note given to his daughter by Fredrick. He'd found it on her bicycle; it stated that he, Frederick, was *sorry*, and he wanted her to *forgive him.* The father had since thrown it away.

Both parents confirmed that Fredrick would occasionally drive their daughter into the fields. She would sit on his lap while he drove. He bought her gifts. He'd bought her the bicycle on which the note for forgiveness had been found. The wife recalled that Fredrick had *Snake Man* on the front of his truck, on a hood mud guard.

When I did a criminal history on Fredrick, I discovered that he'd been convicted in the late 1990s for indecent exposure involving juveniles in a local jurisdiction.

I went to his residence unannounced. His wife answered the door. I introduced myself, and she let me in. I asked her for her husband, and she didn't ask me why. Immediately, I was curious. When a wife doesn't ask me why I want to speak with her husband, I immediately assume she knows why. Fredrick and I made

157

our introductions in his kitchen and his wife walked into the depths of their home. He asked what I wanted, and I, being overly cocky (a mistake), stated that he knew why I was there (*You knew this day was coming*, was what I said to him), but could we talk outside? He readily agreed without further question. He and I spoke on his porch. The wife never came out to sit in on our conversation. She stayed in the house. I never saw her again, never.

As we both sat on his porch overlooking his truck, with *Snake Man* on the hood mud guard, we talked. It was a beautiful spring day.

Fredrick never overtly confessed. He admitted to leaving a note for the girl, apologizing for something he couldn't remember doing. He admitted that he'd let her sit on his lap as he drove the truck. My recording was played in its entirety (all 50 minutes) for the circuit court judge. The defense was trying to argue that I had put words into his client's mouth; he was an uneducated man, and I had manipulated him.

I'll always remember Fredrick for a couple of his profoundly interesting statements: *I'm sorry for whatever I may or may not have done to that little girl.* Rest assured, when he made that statement to me, he clearly knew that I was investigating him for kissing the girl's vagina. The other intriguing statement was: *Maybe what happened was, when I picked her up to kiss her stomach, I may or may not have accidentally touched her privates.*

Really, you accidentally kissed a vagina? As I said before, keep the suspect talking and record him. You never know what he may say.

The judge (presiding over the case) acknowledged that I was obviously more educated than Fredrick and was calculating in how

I interpreted some of his statements and with how I confronted him with them.

The judge even used the word *semantics* prior to his final decision.

Nonetheless, my recording made our conversation very clear. The judge stated that Fredrick had every opportunity to say that he hadn't committed the offense of which he was accused but never did. Although he never confessed to intentionally sodomizing that girl, he did admit that he might have accidentally sodomized her. Fredrick is in prison.

A genuine denial should be timely and with conviction.

Did you do it?

No.

Chapter 55
It should be all about me!

It's just as important to pay attention to the words a victim or witness uses or doesn't use when you're interviewing him. Inadvertent truth can leak out.

When interviewing an alleged victim of a violent crime, I always become curious when the victim refers to the attacker and himself as a **we**. *We got into the car. We went to his house.* That pronoun, *we* implies that you and someone else are together, mutually engaged. *We went on a picnic. We had dinner together.* A victim of a violent crime rarely refers to the actions between he and the attacker with that pronoun, *we. He shoved me into the car; He took me to his house* are valid, victim statements. *He attacked me, and we fought* is also acceptable. *We fought* is a common phrase for two people engaging in a physical struggle. However, I always become intrigued when the victim describes the actions between him and the attacker with that pronoun, *we: We got into the car; we went to his house.* Often, that simple little pronoun, *we*, is an indicator that the victim was complicit in the events being reported. You may want to elicit further information, especially in an alleged rape. Odds are: the victim and the offender have a personal history, a recent history of consensual interaction, when that pronoun *we* is used **often** in a victim's statement.

Words not used are just as important as the words used in a victim's statement. If a victim is very detailed in his description of the events leading up to the alleged crime but lacking in detail with his description of the crime, I, again, become curious. That failure to provide details can indicate a lack of commitment to the words spoken.

I often request a written statement from the victim of an alleged violent crime. I'll preface my request by stating that I understand that he's been through a lot, and I want to spare him from my thousand and one questions. I'll ask that he write down everything he thinks I should know about what happened to him. I'll give him a pad of paper, a pen, and walk away. If he asks where he should start, I'll tell him to start where he thinks he needs to.

Usually, a genuine victim of violence will delve right into the violence; there's very little introduction into why he was where he was and doing what he was doing prior to being victimized. A deceptive person will often describe a lot of reasons why he was there (the place he was victimized) and why he was doing *this or that* prior to whatever he's alleging occurred. A person filing a false report knows that he's being deceptive; so, he'll try to paint a perfect picture; he'll try to lay a good foundation for how and why he became a victim in order to make it believable.

A true victim is telling the truth; so, there's no reason for him to explain why he became a victim. It happened; so, *what's not to believe?*

After reading the victim statement, if I decide that I want more details or clarification about a certain time period of events, I will give the victim a new sheet of paper and make my request for him to write it out.

Do not give the victim his original written statement; otherwise, you'll have cross-outs, erasures, or any other variation of changes that will alter the original wording. You could (and most likely will) lose probative material. As I learned the hard way, the victim could just tear it up or refuse to return that original statement to you. Then, you've got crap.

In 2008, I reviewed a written statement by an alleged rape victim, Jennifer Gordon. There were a lot of concerns: She described her clothes as having been "taken off." Most victims of rape will state that their clothes were *ripped off, torn off, or cut off* (something violent)—not *taken off. Taken off* is a nonviolent term. But the major and most obvious issue was: She'd written a lot of words, over 300, but her entire rape was written as an afterthought: *was forced orally, vaginally, and anally.* In line 47, the last line of her statement, she wrote those words. There'd been no reference to rape or violence until then, line 47. She had stated that a candle and a drink had been knocked over by the side of the bed during some vague reference to a struggle. So, I'll be bold: it doesn't take a rocket scientist to scratch his head and ask the question:

Really, it took you until the last line of your statement to mention the rape?

And (if that wasn't an obvious enough clue) she hadn't used pronouns or any names in those six words. There was a lack of commitment to that last line declaring her rape. It wasn't: He raped me; Johnny raped me; or, I was raped. She allegedly knew the rapist.

Which statement is more committed to the sentiment being expressed, *I love you* or *love you?*

There were some factual inconsistencies with her case that supported my concerns with her written statement; nonetheless, her case was never prosecuted.

> *A victim's statement should revolve predominantly around the actions that occurred against him, not a lot of preamble about what led up to the violence or what happened after the violence. His statement should focus on him and what he experienced (that criminal act against him).*

The violence against me has led me to filing this report.

*There are numerous books on statement analysis. I haven't touched the tip of the iceberg. Read as many books as you can. I will proffer this: the techniques of and insights into statement analysis apply to the verbal narrative. Although I've studied books about statement analysis and have attended some abbreviated trainings, I'm **not** certified in statement analysis. I've simply shared some very useful information.*

Chapter 56
I stepped on a mole, and he told me more

Tunnels go through things—mountains. They go under things—rivers. That's what tunnels do, circumvent obstacles, and people will tunnel through descriptions of things they want to avoid. If a victim or suspect is giving details of an event when, suddenly, those words *and then* or *later* are introduced, it should alert you that something is potentially being left out: potentially something important, something relevant.

Don't let those *tunnels* in time go ignored. Have the person elaborate, fill in those gaps in time. What happened between that one moment and the next? Don't assume.

Our brain is wired to fill in what would seem to be an obvious connection of events. Our brain is continually flooded with billions of pieces of information every second—sight, sound, smell, touch, and taste. It's easier for our brain to make seemingly logical connections than to fully interpret each piece of information and flood our consciousness with each singular sensation and interpretation of that sensation.

When we listen to someone giving an account of events, we'll assume certain connections based on our knowledge of and/or experience with how certain dots are connected.

If someone is recounting his morning from when he woke up until he arrived at work, he might say: *When I woke up around 7:30, I went to the bathroom. I took a shower and brushed my teeth. I got dressed. I had a cup of coffee and drove to work. The traffic, as usual, really sucked. I got to work around 9.*

If I wanted more details, I would employ cognitive interviewing techniques. Cognitive interviewing is essentially about having someone fill in all the little details that the interviewer would otherwise take for granted. A cognitive interviewer never assumes anything. *What kind of toothpaste did you brush your teeth with?*

What woke you up? *The alarm.*

Do you normally get up at 7:30? *Yes.*

Did you do anything before going to the bathroom? *I fed the dog.*

What were you wearing? *Just my underwear.*

What did you do before showing? *I went to the bathroom. I pissed.*

Did you do anything else before getting into the shower? *Oh yeah, my girlfriend called.*

What's her name? *Amber.*

What did you and Amber talk about? *Nothing much.*

What was that nothing? I don't know you or Amber. *She wanted to know where I was last night.*

Where had you been? *At my friend's house.*

What's his name? *John.*

What did you all do? *Hung out.*

What do you mean by hung out? *We drank.*

Anything else? I just need to know everything. You'd forgotten that you had spoken with your girlfriend when you first spoke about what you did that morning. *I was hangin' out with John and some girl.*

What girl? Do you know her name? *Mary.*

Who's Mary? *Just some girl.*

Did you and Mary talk? *Yeah.*

About what? *Stuff.*

What stuff? *Just stuff.*

Do you like Mary? *Kinda.*

Is she cute? *Kinda.*

Did you two do anything? I mean, you're hanging out with John and drinking. Drinking can make us do things we might not otherwise do. You're with a cute girl. *We made out.*

O.K., so, before showering, Amber called. Did she know that you were with Mary? Is that why Amber called? She heard something. She knew about you and Mary. *Yeah.*

I bet she was pissed off? I know how women can be. *Yeah.*

Does Mary know Amber? *Yeah, they are best friends.*

So, you've heard about what happened to Mary then, haven't you? *Yeah.*

What? *She was beat to hell.*

Tell me about Amber's anger issues.

That should give you an idea of why you should never assume connections in a timeline. A little poking and prodding can elicit a lot of information.

It's not just the suspect who'll attempt to deceive law enforcement. People will protect people for a variety of reasons. Keep the line of questioning fluid. Try to elicit information without being accusatory.

Let the suspect keep talking while you guide him down his road of truth.

Chapter 57
Final statement

We want to believe that all people are *capable* of being *as good as we are* while denying that we **aren't as perfect** as we'd like others to believe.

We inherently assume that someone will conduct themselves in a manner consistent with our life experience and education, which is not true. People conduct themselves based on *their life and experiences*, **not** yours.

With everything said, don't ignore the importance of our primitive response to an accusatory question: We omit information and/or lie because we feel threatened. We'll try to protect ourselves; we'll try to save face.

When we deny something we did, our brain interprets that lie as a response to a threat which triggers that medulla oblongata, that primitive portion of our brain. The primitive man was obviously intelligent enough to get us into the twenty-first century, but that primitive man still exists in each and every one of us.

When we lie, he'll creep out to the edge of his cave: scared and unsure (ready to fight or flee). You (as the interrogator) need to guide him completely out of his cave by having him accept the truth (his mistake) with compassionate and nonjudgmental questioning (*keep him from fighting; keep him from running*) in order to keep him **talking**.

The physical and psychological signs of deception are inextricably linked with a person's past, present, and future. We have a need to keep balance; we like to avoid *cognitive dissonance;* we like to alleviate stress; we want to be understood.

We'll tell the truth, if it appears reasonably safe to do so (if we feel safe with the person before us).

Please continue to go to training, read books, and watch others. Review your own interviews and interrogations—the successful and unsuccessful; I learn more from my unsuccessful ones. Accept that no one, not even you (not even the badge), is perfect.

Your own mind is the most important maze to crawl into... before you crawl into another's.

Most importantly, be safe.

Chapter 58
References and/or personal recommendations (fiction and non-fiction)

American Psychiatric Association, *Diagnostic and Statistical Manual of Mental Disorders (Fourth Edition)* (American Psychiatric Association, 1400 K Street, N.W., Washington, DC 20005, 1994).

Gavin de Becker, *The Gift of Fear* (New York: Dell, 1998).

Douglas J. Besharov, *Recognizing Child Abuse, A Guide for the Concerned* (New York: The Free Press, a division of Macmillan, 1990).

John C. Bowden, *An Investigator's Guide to Interviews & Interrogation* (Duncan, OK 73534: APTAC Publications, 2009).

Peter Breggin, M.D., *Toxic Psychiatry* (New York: St. Martin's Press, 1991).

Dale Carnegie, *How to Win Friends & Influence People* (New York: Pocket Books, a division of Simon & Schuster, 1936).

Ted Conover, *New Jack (Guarding Sing Sing)* (New York: Vintage Books, a division of Random House, 2001).

Michael Crichton, *Eaters of the Dead* (New York: HarperCollins, 1976).

Paul Ekman, *Emotions Revealed, Recognizing Faces and Feelings to Improve Communication and Emotional Life* (New York: Holt Paperbacks/Henry Holt and Company, 2003).

Paul Ekman and Wallace V. Friesen, *Unmasking the Face, A Guide to Recognizing Emotions from Facial Expressions* (Cambridge, MA: Malor Books, 2003).

Marc Galanter, *Cults (Faith, Healing, and Coercion)* (New York: Oxford University Press, 1989).

Robert D. Hare, Ph.D., *Without Conscience, The Disturbing World of the Psychopaths Among Us* (New York: The Guilford Press, 1993).

Stephen W. Hawking, *A Brief History of Time* (New York: A Bantam Book, 1988).

Jonathan Kellerman, *Savage Spawn, Reflections on Violent Children* (New York: The Ballantine Publishing Group, a division of Random House, 1999).

Steven D. Levitt & Stephen J. Dubner, *Freakonomics, A Rogue Economist Explores the Hidden Side of Everything* (New York: HarperCollins, 2005).

James Allan Matte, *Forensic Psychophysiology Using the Polygraph (Scientific Truth Verification—Lie Detection)* (New York: J.A.M. Publication, 1993).

Debbie Nathan & Michael Snedeker, *Satan's Silence, Ritual Abuse and the Making of a Modern American Witch Hunt* (New York: BasicBooks, a division of HarperCollins Publishers, 1995).

Gary Noesner, *Stalling for Time, My Life as an FBI Hostage Negotiator* (New York: Random House Publishing Group, 2010).

John O'Brien, *Leaving Las Vegas* (New York: Grove Press, 1990).

Allan and Barbara Pease, *The Definitive Book of Body Language* (New York, New York: Bantam Dell, a division of Random House, 2004).

Robert M. Persig, *Zen and The Art of Motorcycle Maintenance* (New York: A Bantam Book/published by arrangement with William Morrow and Company, 1974).

Mary Pipher, Ph.D., *Reviving Ophelia, Saving the Selves of Adolescent Girls* (New York: Ballantine Books, a division of Random House, 1994).

Katherine Ramsland, *The Forensic Psychology of Criminal Minds* (New York: The Berkley Publishing group, Published by Penguin group, 2010).

Diane Ravitch, *The Language Police: How Pressure Groups Restrict What Students Learn* (New York: Knopf, 2003).

John E. Reid & Associates, *The Reid Technique of Interviewing and Interrogation* (209 West Jackson Boulevard, Suite 400, Chicago, IL 60606, 2006).

Wendell C. Rudacille, *Identifying Lies in Disguise* (Dubuque, Iowa: Kendall/Hunt Publishing Company, 1994).

Anna C. Salter, Ph.D., *Predators (Pedophiles, Rapists, & Other Sex Offenders)* (New York: Basic Books, 2003).

174

Stanton E. Samenow, Ph.D., *Inside the Criminal Mind* (New York: Times Books, a division of Random House, 1984).

Saphire/Ramona Lofton, *Push* (New York: Vintage Books, a division of Random House, 1996).

Sally Satel M.D., *PC M.D. How Political Correctness is Corrupting Medicine* (New York: Basic Books, 2001).

Hubert Selby Jr., *Last Exit to Brooklyn* (New York: Grove Press, 1994).

Donna Rae Siegfried, *Anatomy & Physiology for Dummies* (New York: Wiley Publishing, 2002).

Naomi Wolf, *Promiscuities, The Secret Struggle for Womanhood* (New York: Random House, 1997).

Richard Wrangham & Dale Peterson, *Demonic Males, Apes and the Origins of Human Violence* (New York: Houghton Mifflin Company, 1996).

Koren Zailckas, *A Story of a Drunken Girlhood* (New York: Penguin Books, 2006).

Index